D1590040

# BETWIXT HEAVEN AND CHARING CROSS

# Betwixt Heaven and Charing Cross

## The Story of St. Martin-in-the-Fields

CAROLYN SCOTT

ROBERT HALE · LONDON

*First published in Great Britain 1971*

ISBN 0 7091 2158 X

Robert Hale & Company
63 Old Brompton Road
London S.W.7



PRINTED AND BOUND IN GREAT BRITAIN
BY C. TINLING AND CO. LTD
LONDON AND PRESCOT

The angels keep their ancient places;—
Turn but a stone, and start a wing!
'Tis ye, 'tis your estrangéd faces,
That miss the many splendoured thing.

But (when so sad thou canst not sadder)
Cry;—and upon thy so sore loss
Shall shine the traffic of Jacob's ladder
Pitched betwixt Heaven and Charing Cross.

Yea, in the night, my Soul, my daughter,
Cry,—clinging Heaven by the hems;
And lo, Christ walking on the water,
Not of Gennesareth, but Thames!

Francis Thompson

## AUTHOR'S NOTE

St. Martin's is continually on the move, changing as people change, adapting to suit new situations and meet new needs. The people and the situations described in this book are part of that moving pattern. The people will change, the situations develop and progress, but the basis of the pattern remains the same.

All royalties earned by the sale of this book will go to St. Martin-in-the-Fields.

## CONTENTS

# ILLUSTRATIONS

## PICTURE CREDITS

Radio Times Hulton Picture Library: 3, 4; Guildhall Library: 6; North Thames Gas Board: 9, 10, 11; Houston Rogers: 13; Desmond O'Neill: 15; Planet News: 16; Sport and General Agency: 17; Romano Cagnoni: 18, 23, 24, 25, 26; Topix: 19; Syndication International: 21.

CHAPTER ONE

# THE CHURCH IN THE SQUARE

St. Martin-in-the-Fields is the royal parish church. It has been called the parish church of the Commonwealth. It is in all the guide books. It is also the first thing you see when you wake in the morning if you sleep out at night in Trafalgar Square.

"Like a broken love affair. . . ." That is how one man felt when he left the staff of St. Martin's recently. He couldn't explain why. The only explanation was to watch and look and listen.

"Sure and someone pinched me shoes again. Now what can I do about that?" A hot Sunday afternoon, the white of the steps dusty in the sunshine. Paddy the Irishman, up from the Reception Centre in Peckham, eyeing the railings above the social service unit before padding down to the crypt below the church for a cardboard cup of soup.

The square, full of tourists and pigeons and protest banners, crumbs and ice-cream papers trodden underfoot. Balloons being let off from the church steps to celebrate the start of a campaign to feed the hungry, and the Mayor of Westminster making a speech standing by a boy asleep in the sun.

And downstairs in the crypt, more chaotic than Piccadilly Circus underground, everything taking place at once, rather like a miracle. An African dance group rehearsing the drums. The Chinese congregation with scores of Chinese children running up and down the uneven stone passages. Queues at the soup kitchen and the smell of soup. The Folk Club tea and the Alcoholics Anonymous groups.

Prayers for peace in the church upstairs, with the doors wide open and police sirens sounding in the square. Straw hats and prayer books, summer dresses and someone asleep, and the blue cross in the altar window changing colour as it loses sight of the sun. Reuben from Barbados carrying the cross. Little old Jessie, scuttling across the chancel as she always does, to take a closer look at the preacher, and Moses with the beard, divested of his sandwich boards, waving and calling, "Thanks very much!" as he leaves the communion rail. A tourist asking if this goddam place is Westminster Abbey.

Night-time, and the black of the sky and the white of the church. Someone in search of a bed for the night, and temporary, tentative silence.

It is said that St. Martin is not only the patron saint of reformed drinkers. He is also the patron saint of drunks. He gave half his cloak to a beggar. Since the days when Charles II worshipped in the church and Nell Gwynne was buried in the vaults, St. Martin's has been no respecter of persons. In a haphazard way, it tries to respect everyone. The African who says, "without St. Martin's I'd be dead", and the dosser coming a long way back to return the razor blades he didn't use. The man who slept the night under the altar and came back next morning for his gloves. Kevin, on heroin and slowly going to rack and ruin, always beside him, with no future whatever, his girlfriend Ann. The boy called Jesus, bone idle and beautiful; and Nellie, washing her under-clothes in the crypt toilet, flushing her stockings down and getting them stuck and causing untold complications.

Tolerance and tension, creative and unpredictable. A little, as he said, like a love affair.

CHAPTER TWO

# SUDDEN SUNSHINE...

Seven hundred and fifty years ago there was no sound but the song of birds and wind on the water where the sirens and the clamour of starlings shatter the peace today.

A windmill stood in Windmill Street, and children ran barefoot along the beaches of the Strand where the river turned by the village with the wooden cross called Charing. And monks, begging halfpennies on their way from St. Peter's Abbey to a day's work in the Convent Gardens, stopped to count their cash and say their offices at the tiny chapel of St. Martin-nigh-the-Cross.

St. Martin was a soldier and a saint. He became Bishop of Tours. But none of these has very much impact today. Learned men have argued the toss whether or not Martin was a pacifist, whether or not he gave his blessing to drinking and debauchery, but these don't seem to matter. It is a single action, one winter night riding towards the city gates of Amiens, that has caught and held the imagination. When St. Martin was a soldier, he gave half his cloak to a beggar, and as he went to sleep that night, he dreamed that the beggar was Christ.

It is this that seems to matter today more than anything else. And perhaps it matters too, that when the sun shines in November, it is called St. Martin's Summer. Because as you trace the story of St. Martin's since that first chapel in the meadows, you will occasionally stumble on the sunshine of an unexpected summer.

The first was in 1543. Plague had hit London again, carried by fleas in the big black rats brought to England by merchant ships from the East. Yards were piled high with bodies, and grave-diggers had little time to spare for philosophy. Parsons burned the wick low writing laboriously in the parish registers, cramming the names together to save space on the expensive parchment. Entire families appear one after another in a matter of days, all accorded the letter *P* after their name. *P* stood for Plague.

St. Martin-nigh-the-Cross had become a parish church in its own right. Parish duties had increased from the capture of hedgehogs and the care of cows to include the imposition of taxes and the upkeep of the one main high road. Because Queen Ann Boleyn had been offended by the sight of bodies taken past the Palace of Whitehall from the houses in the North of the parish of St. Margaret's to be buried at the Westminster church, the district had been annexed to St. Martin's, and the white-washed chapel in the meadows with its small, square tower and floor of coloured tiles had been replaced by a larger, brick-built church with an Italian style bell-tower. Built up from the ground on the original foundations because it was cheaper and easier that way, the new church was a community effort. Parishioners were poor. Apart from the bishop and a few noblemen with houses by the river, where their barges were moored down the steps by the water-gates to the Thames, there were only the scattered homes of the workmen. And it was the workmen who came with their gifts of iron and flint and chalk and lead for the roof and carts piled high with stone.

But by the time the bells were hung and the church was finished, it was no longer a time for rejoicing.

The Vicar of St. Martin's, the Reverend Robert Best, was as busy as the rest of the clergy. There were over 100 births a month, and as many deaths. There was the baby found crying in the corner of the yard in front of the new church. He had christened the child John Churchyard. And little Elizabeth Pall Mall, hidden away under a stall in the street. He paid for their food and clothing until better arrangements could be made. Friends scoffed at him for being stupid, but he wasn't stupid. He knew that better arrangements never would be made. They were a wild hope for the future.

The Plague increased. The entries became more numerous, more crammed together. Already Robert Best was stretching his resources to pay the funeral expenses of the penniless women found dead in the fields and the foundlings who died begging in the streets. But he knew it wasn't enough. There seemed little point in helping people who were already dead.

Soon, there were more entries in the book:

"Buried a poor child from the Vicarage.
Buried a poor woman from the Vicarage."

Both had died from the Plague.

It is hard to imagine the dilemma he faced before he decided to risk infecting his own household so that a few peasants could die with a measure of decency and dignity. All we do know is that where today a twenty-four hour social service unit operates, over 400 years ago, a clergyman called Robert Best and his two curates began the first twenty-four hour social service unit by bringing penniless people sick with the Plague back across the fields to the vicarage so that they could die with a roof over their heads and a little privacy and peace.

When the Plague ended, sweet herbs were strewn in the church, and the perfume hung above the altar. The altar itself, and the props that surrounded it, were constantly changing. Crosses and candlesticks and missals were bought and sold and the rood screen taken up and put down again. The Lord's Prayer and the ten commandments were painted on the walls and then whitewashed over. Queen Mary Tudor attended sung Mass. Four years later, Queen Elizabeth ordered that services should be said in English instead of in Latin. In the end the clergy, some in confusion, others in defiance, went their own way. Some took their services strictly according to the Prayer Book; others extemporised. Some had an altar in the body of the church; others had it placed high up in the chancel. Some wore surplices and some did not. The strange institution of the Thirty-Nine Articles was brought in as a fraught attempt to regularise the situation, and St. Martin's churchwardens pointedly invested in an hour glass. The vicar frequently interrupted his sermon to ask members of the congregation to snore more quietly as the sand had not yet run its course. If he was still preaching when the sands ran out, the people got up and went home.

By the turn of the century, when Dr. Thomas Mountforde was vicar, the work of caring for the people who could not care for themselves was well underway. At Christmas time and at Easter gifts of bread and beef were distributed to the parish poor, and orphans had their shirts and their smocks, their shoes and aprons paid for by the church. A boy called Ben Jonson attended the St. Martin's school for poor boys because his stepfather was a bricklayer and his home by Charing Cross was a poor one. Church funds were still coping with the upkeep of John Churchyard: his new coat cost 1s. 5d. Already men were coming down from the North to London only to find that the streets were not after all paved with gold. Pennies were paid out to men and women in the streets and to strangers from abroad. Elevenpence for a lame woman from Drury Lane, 5d. for a woman selling milk in the street, and 11d. for a shroud to bury a blackamoor who died at Thameside. Doctors and surgeons were sent to help the sick, treatments and diets were paid for out of church funds, and water was carried to the houses of people too sick to fetch water for themselves. King James gave an acre of land, and as people continued to move into London, the church was enlarged and charity houses built on the gardens that surrounded it.

Congregations grew. And in spite of liberal sprinkling with holy water from horse-hair brushes and 2d. worth of fresh herbs on Sundays, it was perhaps as well that even then, the doors were always open.

"The malt duty", wrote a newspaper called the *London Spy*, in the seventeenth century, "is nowhere better promoted

"Pitched betwixt Heaven and Charing Cross"

Evelyn the diarist wrote of Archbishop Tenison, appointed Vicar of St. Martin's in 1680: "I esteem him to be one of the most profitable preachers in the Church of England"

than in this part of town." It was referring to the quantities of beer drunk in St. Martin's Lane. At the same time, rails were erected round the altar inside the church, "to prevent persons sitting on it, throwing hats on it, writing on it, and abusing it to other profaner uses". The King, scattering hempseed for the ducks on the canal, forgot that there were no longer any ducks on it, and the delighted poor quarrelled and scrapped over the unexpected largesse. Children sat for hours screaming at the antics of Punchinello thwacking his wife in a gaudy little booth by Charing Cross.

Dr. Thomas Tenison was Vicar of St. Martin's; and at a time when the church was very much the church of the aristocracy, housing five earls within its parish boundaries, he was an unusual man.

He was independent. Incensed when the King stole his prerogative by appointing a church lecturer, Tenison insisted on his rights to appoint a man himself. When the King apologised and withdrew, Tenison accepted the apology, was satisfied that he had made his point, and immediately reinstated the King's man.

He was renowned as a priest. Stories of his understanding and his kindness with the sick or the sinning were so widely told that a man high-jacked into executing Charles I begged him to come and hear his confession and give him absolution before he died.

He was astute. When his curates spent too many hours idling in the coffee-houses and clubs, he set them the task of collecting and cataloguing one of the first London libraries. And because he was no narrow ascetic, he insisted that the collection should include books of wide general interest as well as books on theology and divinity.

And he was far-sighted. Huguenot immigrants from France were welcomed into the parish and the skills they brought with them were quickly absorbed. Dent the watchmaker opened his own shop, and so did Vaillant the bookseller. Le Beck began a restaurant in Bedford Street, and a rich and colourful silk market grew up around Charing Cross.

Although the Huguenots built their own chapel, St. Martin's gave hospitality to their new neighbours, and then allowed them to be buried in the parish burial grounds. Artists and silversmiths settled down to create and to teach, and a new kind of beauty entered the scene. A French engraver became principal of the school which was later to become the Royal Academy. A Frenchman married and had a son who became a churchwarden at St. Martin's church.

But above all, Tenison was a philanthropist—with his heart and the money at his disposal. He wanted to help poor people to better themselves. His library was to be the first lending library in Westminster, and to subsidise it, he put a levy on the rates. When the library was underway, he started two schools for the children of the poor, one in Leicester Square and the other in Charing Cross Road. More than anything else, he wanted poor people to be able to read and to write and to understand things for themselves without relying on a priest to translate their letters and fill up their forms.

"It's not their place to be educated," was the reaction of the rich, who didn't take kindly to a levy on their rates. But the ruling of Westminster was carried out by the church from the vestry hall where the royal coat of arms hung, and they had no alternative.

But there is one side of Tenison's character which endears him more than all the rest. Along the Strand from St. Martin's, to many raised eyebrows and the scandalised comments of the reactionaries, plays were being put on at the Theatre Royal Drury Lane. One night, a girl with long red hair playing the part of a street girl selling oranges caught the eye of the King. Her name was Nell Gwynne.

Nell lived in the parish of St. Martin's, and if Dr. Tenison had a sense of humour, it must have amused him to see her, with her loving and her laughing and her open heart, winning almost without trying, the affections of all but the primmest of his parishioners. And she was generous with more than her affections. The money she gave to the poor, she gave more gladly than the aristocracy paid their paupers' rates. He liked Nell. And he probably thought that Christ would have liked her too.

Perhaps, after the King's death, when Nell, finding it hard to change her ways, was poor again and only just able to make ends meet on the erratic allowances made to her by King James, Tenison paid his parish visits to the house at 79 Pall Mall. Perhaps he took tea or drank port in the magnificent drawing room full of mirrors. But when Nell died before she was 40 years old, her final request caused a furore.

She left £100 to the parish poor, asked that she should be buried in St. Martin's, and that her friend, Dr. Tenison, should preach a sermon at her funeral.

"If she wants to be buried at St. Martin's, she shall be buried at St. Martin's," was the only comment the Vicar made to his indignant parishioners. Then he preached a sermon praising Nell's generosity, her kindness and her open heart, and settled the matter by having her buried in the vicar's vault.

CHAPTER THREE

# ... AND UNEXPECTED SUMMERS

"I think the full tide of human existence is at Charing Cross," said Dr. Johnson, as he walked down from a meal at the Pine Apple Tavern in New Street. But the full tide of human existence was kept firmly outside the doors of St. Martin's.

A kind of unity had been achieved by James Gibbs, the architect of the new church, gleaming bright and white in the sunshine. He had placed a contemporary Western spire on top of a pillared portico which echoed the lines of an ancient Greek temple, and the result, completed in 1726, was being busily praised and ridiculed. But there the unity ended. Inside the church, rented pews could cost as much as £10 a year, and charity children sat in the box especially built for them, high up at the west end of the church.

Trumpets sounded and people cheered as the foundation stone of the new church was laid five years earlier in the name of King George I. Buffalo heads were dug up beneath the ground where the old church had been, and workmen received a purse of 100 guineas as a present from the King. Sir James, a pupil of Christopher Wren, was so intent on perfection that he sacked the bricklayer and the clerk of works for using inferior bricks, and work started all over again.

The font from the old church, where Charles II had been baptised, was kept and replaced in the back of the new church. The steeple was built by Master Mason Christopher Cass, who belonged to the Company of Masons whose spires are still standing 250 years and two world wars later. Grinling Gibbons carved the intricate, high pulpit, with its cleanly sweeping staircase. Quartered lilies of France decorated the royal arms carved over the chancel, and chairs of cedar wood sent as a gift from His Majesty's Governor in South Carolina and designed by Gibbs himself, were placed by a great fire-place in the royal pews. King George became so enthused with the project that he took the unprecedented action of becoming the first and only monarch to hold the position of a churchwarden.

Wide Corinthian columns on high pedestals supported the elliptical ceiling—"much better for the voice", according to Gibbs—which was designed in gold-embellished mouldings and bosses on a pale blue-green background by two famous Italian artists, Artari and Bagutti. Outside, above the double flight of wide steps, the ornate pillared portico was so much admired that when an architect was commissioned to plan the building of the National Gallery it was stipulated that he must on no account block the view of St. Martin's portico from Pall Mall.

Chippendale, from his family workshop in St. Martin's Lane, worshipped at the new church and was buried there. So was Jack Sheppard the highwayman, Hilliard the painter and Roubillac the sculptor. Samuel Dunce married Clara Pigg and William Shirt married Mary Cotton, and the water-men plying their boats like taxis from watergate to watergate along the Strand, claimed the privilege of being buried in the watermen's churchyard, where today the buses run into Duncannon Street.

A stuntman tied a rope from the church tower to the Royal Mews opposite and descended it head first. Encouraged by an enthusiastic reception he tried the same thing again at another church and died when the rope broke and he fell to the ground. Stone urns placed round the top ledge of the body of the church were removed after one of them fell down on top of a passer-by. St. Martin's, even in the eighteenth century, was uneasy about gimmicks.

The bells which had once rung before all the rest in London to tell the glad tidings of the defeat of the Armada were now recast, and with new bells added, they became one of the finest twelve bell peals in London. The Lords of the

Admiralty who had adopted the church as their own, gave a royal standard to be flown on great occasions, and the bells rang and the flag fluttered for the victories of Trafalgar and Waterloo. One Sunday morning a stranger from abroad, penniless and homesick in London, heard the bells of St. Clement's and St. Martin's pealing out together as he walked along the Strand, and the clatter carried on the sunshine reminded him of orange and lemon groves in Italy and bells ringing on the hillsides at home.

On Sunday afternoons, people crowded into the church to hear the famous composer Handel play the Voluntary on an organ built by the King's organ-builder at the cost of £1,500 given by the King, and containing three miles of tubing. "The inhabitants are now supplied with a decent tabernacle," sniped a London paper. "A tabernacle which can produce as handsome a show of white hands, diamond rings, pretty snuff-boxes and gilt prayer books as any cathedral whatever. Here the fair penitents pray in their patches, sue for pardon in their paint and see their heaven in man."

But there were also the famous poor. Up in St. Martin's Lane where the philosophers and poets and painters sat, Samuel Johnson exercised his own kind of thrift. "I dined very well," he said, "for eightpence, with very good company. It used to cost the rest one shilling, for they drank wine; but I had a cut of meat for sixpence and bread for one penny, and gave the waiter one penny: so I was quite as well served, nay better than the rest, for they gave the waiter nothing."

Such consideration was rare. For a small fee, sightseers could spend a long time laughing at the mad inmates of the Stone Hospital opposite Charing Cross, and only complained when the building was moved to make way for the new promenade, to be called Trafalgar Square. Which, as it turned out, was probably one of the most jerry-built tourist traps in the world.

To accommodate it, St. Martin's had to sacrifice its front yard. Nelson's column was built 14 feet too high, and his statue was already strapped up and ready to be hoisted on top before the mistake was realised. The artist Landseer walked out and died of drink before his lions could be finished, and when at last they were ready and put in place thirty years later, the people pelted them with stones. The fountains which today run with pink ink or froth with detergent on high days and holidays, leaked almost before they had water in them, and a special well to supply them had to be sunk as a hurried afterthought.

Then, at last, when the final wooden bricks had been laid and the steps completed, the fiasco became fashionable.

But St. Martin's, even then, had a certain unpredictability.

One Good Friday, a man with a sword rushed through the door of the church into the middle of the congregation. He was running away from the bailiffs, and the only safe place he knew was St. Martin's. Several years later, a man walked into the church during the evening service and fired two shots at the priest. He had been cheated of more than £100 by his landlord, and the shock had confused him so much that he could no longer distinguish his friends from his enemies. But if disturbances in church are no new thing, neither is tolerance and a sense of immediacy. In 1815, a St. Martin's Vicar called Joseph Potts succeeded in raising over £13,000 for soldiers wounded at Waterloo. Years later, almshouses were built for the church at Camden Town. They were to be for any woman resident within the ancient boundaries of St. Martin's parish who was unable to support herself.

They were to be allocated regardless of religious creed.

Like love and hate, tolerance and intolerance walked out together hand in hand. Scavenging in and out of the crowded stalls of Hungerford Market by Charing Cross, a ragged boy called Charles Dickens observed one of the church's most obvious intolerances. Strutting in scarlet greatcoat with gold lace cuffs—which cost the church £13—and large three-cornered cocked hat trimmed with gold—which cost the church £3 10s.—the parish beadle paraded with his silver cane. Serving summonses for rent arrears and barring ragamuffins from church services, it would have taken more than flattery and a drop of gin with a lump of sugar in it to persuade him, as Mr. Bumble was fleetingly persuaded, that even beadles were but men.

But times were changing. The last reference to payment for a beadle's uniform appeared in St. Martin's accounts for 1858. Gas, an innovation first tried out at Carlton House and to light the street of Pall Mall, was brought into the church to replace oil and candles. Towards the end of the century, St. Martin's became the first London church to have electric light installed. The vaults, already overcrowded with more than 3,000 coffins crammed into them, were cleared and the bodies removed to the farthest vaults and to Camden Town cemetery. After years of inadequate burials in wooden coffins, the sight that lay behind the barred iron gates was a pungent one of change and decay.

> On going down below the church we found ourselves in the crypt [wrote Frank Buckland, a historian]. This crypt is supported by massive pillars, and the spaces between some of them are bricked up so as to form vaults, some large and some small. There are the rector's vaults, the portico vault, and the steeple vault, as well as several smaller vaults taken by private families. The larger vaults were guarded by strong iron gates, through which the coffins could be seen from the outside. Having unlocked the ponderous oak doors of the vault number three, we threw the light of our bull's-eye lanterns into the vault, and then I beheld a sight I shall never forget. After our eyes had got accustomed to the light, we perceived that this vault was a good-sized room, as full as it ever could hold with coffins, piled one over the other, from the very top to the very bottom. Many coffins were even piled up crosswise in front of the door, so that no entry could be obtained except by moving them, and others were jammed up together in all possible positions, without the least attempt at order, reminding one much of books packed in a box to be sent away. To the left of this vault there began another, in which there was a great mass of wooden coffins of persons buried anterior to the Act which ordered that no person should be buried there except in lead.

The faint and sickly effluvia which emanated from these was truly overpowering and poisonous.

King George IV gave ground for the building of a charity school, vicarage and vestry hall, by the side of the church, and in 1830 it was opened. Over 100 years later, Ian Nairn wrote of it: "This poignant stucco façade at the back of St. Martin's announces one of London's loveliest buildings. In mist or rain it will never let you down; and the glint of sunshine on the pilasters puts daggers straight into your guts. This is the kernel of London, an epitome of what makes cockneys homesick."

In 1871, at St. Martin's church, Captain Bates married Ann Swann. It was a June wedding and the sun shone. Both bride and groom were over 7 feet high, and when Captain Bates stepped into his carriage, his boots went straight through the floor.

A list of the men who have been Vicar of St. Martin's hangs above the stairway to the North Gallery. It is a long list of forgotten names.

Robert Best, committed to Newgate Prison for singing the litany in English to his peasant congregation. William Lloyd, vicar in 1676, sent to the Tower of London by King James II for refusing to publish and distribute the King's Declaration in his church. Dr. Tenison, of whom Evelyn wrote in his diary, "I esteem him to be one of the most profitable preachers in the Church of England. The pains he takes, and care of his parish will, I fear, wear him out, which would be an inexpressible loss"; who revised the Prayer Book, largely according to his own inclinations. Dr. Lancaster, vicar from 1692, succeeding through his own unquenchable enthusiasm, in collecting enough money to start a charity school in the parish. Dr. Hamilton, vicar from 1776 to 1812, trying to infuse compassion into the system by waiving his burial fee for the parish poor, and retaliating to a back-dated rates claim for £54 by claiming fees of £850 for the 4,544 pauper burials he had conducted free of charge since his induction.

And at the end of the nineteenth century, in the vicarage dining room, William Humphrey, Vicar of St. Martin's from 1855 to 1886, lending his mind and his imagination to a committee bent on revising the New Testament. Obsessed, like so many Vicars of St. Martin's, with the need to let a glimpse of summer sunshine into the dark and creaking machinery of the Church, he found his glorious summer faced too often not by a winter of discontent, but of vested interest, apathy and a certain suspicion.

The names mean nothing today. Nothing except the memory of a man who became a dean or a bishop or an archbishop to have his name painted up on a board in gold. And yet each name held its own spring and its own winter, and its own personal unexpected summer.

It was summertime in 1886, when a young man in a threadbare coat stood in the gutter outside St. Martin's selling matches. His name was Francis Thompson. He was 26 years old, a poet and an opium addict. He had lived in doss houses for 5d. a cabin, and when his money ran out he had spent the nights huddled in doorways, moved on by police, falling asleep at last on the wet grass of Green Park at four in the morning. "Were not sleep as brief as deep," he wrote, "it were better almost to die than sleep."

John McMaster, a churchwarden at St. Martin's, passed Thompson many times. At last, he took him in and tried to teach him the bootmaking trade at his shop in Panton Street. Thompson began to grow a little better, and he began to write again. Then addiction caught up with him, and McMaster told him he must go. The glimpse of affection and small security snatched away, bewildered and alone, the young poet spent his last halfpenny on two boxes of matches and went out into the street, walking along the gutter in the shadow of the church, trying to sell them.

He was one of the first of the disillusioned, searching in his own way for a sight of Jacob's ladder pitched between Heaven and Charing Cross. John McMaster, zealous, inadequate and awkward, was one of the first people to try to help.

CHAPTER FOUR

# AMELIA

"When I first came here, these rooms cost two shillings a week. Now, they cost ten. A quarter of tea was fourpence, and there were bundles of turnips for twopence and big brown stone jars of pickles and jam at the market place for sixpence-halfpenny. I can remember my mother buying coal, a hundredweight of best Silkstone for elevenpence."

Amelia Purcell is 92. She came to the Peabody Buildings in the Bedfordbury Estate behind St. Martin's Lane when she was 3 years old, and still lives in the same rooms she and her eight brothers and sisters were brought up in. The Buildings haven't changed much. Water still has to be fetched from the cold tap on the landing and heated on the stove. Lavatories are still communal. The blocks are still known uncompromisingly as A, B, C, D and E Block. One or two children play in the yard, but most young families have moved on. Change has taken place outside rather than inside. Except for the sound of television echoing down the stone stairs.

Amelia is quiet and courteous and constantly surprised at the number of people who love to visit her. She has probably lived in the parish longer than anyone else, and her memory is clear as daylight.

"Opposite Bedfordbury there used to be courts with little cottages one storey high and attics where they grew geraniums. You went up one step into the parlour. Turner's Court was right opposite our gate. All the pickpockets lived there, and when the police blew their whistles you'd see a man disappear through Turner's Court and soon afterwards he'd be out in St. Martin's Lane. They dug underground tunnels from house to house. We were always warned not to go out in the road. There were railings and a gate to keep us in the yard. We weren't allowed to walk on that side of the road.

"There were shops and houses where the Coliseum is now. And between Mays Buildings and Hop Gardens, there was the little church of the Good Shepherd. That was our church. We could come out of the back door of the Buildings and there in front of us was the stone statue of the Good Shepherd carrying a lamb. It wasn't licensed for marriages, but there was a stone font, and we had baptisms. There was an old-fashioned organ and the organist used to sit pumping it at Sunday School with all the boys sitting beside him. Mr. Gladstone used to go there. He liked the little church.

"We didn't often go to St. Martin's. I remember school prize-givings there. I went to the National School by the church, and I won a prize when I was six years old, and when I looked up at the Vicar, his beard tickled my forehead.

"The pews were all locked in those days. They were kept for the rich people from Carlton House Terrace and St. James's Square. They were family pews. Each one had a number, and we couldn't go into them. But we could walk down each side, or sit on the rush chairs in the middle. I remember sitting on the rush chairs when I was very little. The verger had a cane to keep us quiet.

"We used to spend hours gazing at the Ascension window over the altar. It was an enormous full-size figure of Our Lord blessing his disciples, and we used to try and guess which was Peter and which was John by the expression on their faces. They were all there, kneeling and looking up.

"It was a very fashionable church. The rich people came in their carriages with their coachmen and footmen, and when the new vicar came he had eight children and a cook and a complete staff of servants, and they had to build a top floor onto the vicarage for him. There was the vicarage mews where his carriage was kept. The coachman lived over the mews, and there was a terrace where all the other coachmen lived, with stables below for their broughams. There were stables where they take scenery into the Coliseum now, and you could hear the cock crowing in the morning, over at Buer's Yard where they kept the carthorses. And all day you could hear them at Charing Cross station, whistling for cabs from the rank in Agar Street.

"There were five shops in Bedfordbury—an oil shop, a stationer, a butcher, a baker and a gentleman's tailor, and then Toole's Theatre where Irene and Violet Vanbrugh acted. They were the sisters of a clergyman. The stage door was opposite our window and we used to watch the musicians and actors coming out and talking round the door until they were called.

"St. Martin's Lane was known as Dentists' Row in those days. False teeth had just come in, and you passed window after window of dentures. We children used to stand at the windows and gaze at them with our hands over our mouths. We were afraid they'd come and take our teeth and put them in the window.

"A penny to a child then—it was like a shilling! We'd buy a farthing's worth of sweets, and we were given a lot for a farthing. The older girls from school used to come to the rag shop with a pile of old copy books, and then when you bought a halfpenny-worth of pickles or two-penny-worth of butter, your butter would be wrapped in the paper the children had written their copy lines on. You could buy jam from the chandlers in a sugar loaf bag made out of a copy book—a big ladle of jam for twopence.

"Parents paid weekly to send children to the National School. It cost 2d. a week in the first year, 3d. in the second, then 4d. and 6d. for the top class. That was before there was a School Board for London. They were church schools, and the teachers were employed by the vicar. When people were very poor, he helped them. It could mean a lot of money to pay out for a large family.

"But even in those days, the vicars were always very attentive to the poor people. They looked after them even if they didn't come to church. There were mothers' meetings, and the Band of Hope, and there were needlework classes in the evenings for coster women from the corner street to learn to make their white aprons. And there were classes for the flower women who sold buttonholes, and the step-women who cleaned the shops.

"Children had a lot of illnesses then. It was quite ordinary to hear them calling out, 'Here's the fever cart!' Then you'd see a little child being carried down in a blanket. I was taken away once with scarlet fever. The van was pulled by horses, and you had to step up into the back of it. I can remember those words so often, called through the railings as we played hop scotch or skipping rope: 'Here's the fever cart!'

"And there were the big, open-work gates that were always kept locked. We thought there must be ghosts down there. They were on the left of the church above the stone steps down to the mortuary. When people drowned on the river we used to see the bodies carried down the steps.

"But everyone shared everything then. You shared one another's troubles and pleasures. When a child died, the other children took some flowers and went to see the little one in the coffin. There was no fear. And a marriage or a birthday was like a family event. Sometimes we had to set up tables in the laundry because there were so many people. And in the summer we had parties in the yard outside the Buildings.

"It was summer in 1914 when I saw the boys all resting in the church courtyard after walking miles from the country to enlist. They looked too young to be soldiers.

"It was about that time when Mr. Sheppard came."

CHAPTER FIVE

# THE IMPATIENT PARSON

When Dick Sheppard first came to look at St. Martin's, he found one thing that attracted him. "I sat in the empty church for a long time," he said later. "And the only sound I could hear—to me a strangely hopeful one—was the noise of the busy world outside, punctuated by children's voices in the churchyard."

Later, he explored the parish. He talked to patients in the casualty department of Charing Cross Hospital. He spoke to the people who lived in the courts of Bedfordbury. He visited the public houses and the shops and the hostels, and when night came, he carried on visiting. The only people still out on the streets in Piccadilly and by the river were the people with no home to go to, and he sat on benches with them and talked to them until he ended up in the early morning, with coffee and a bun from a stall by the church, sitting on the parapet of the National Gallery, watching the dawn break.

"That night's impressions", he said, "persuaded me that no square mile could provide a more thrilling or adventurous pitch."

But the year was 1914. While soldiers continued to queue in the churchyard waiting to enlist, far away in the fields of Flanders, the war they dreamed of winning was being fought. Dick Sheppard accepted the post of Vicar of St. Martin-in-the-Fields and then went for three months to the Front as a chaplain. He was 34.

"I think the memory of those months haunted him all his life," says someone who knew him then. "When he was well, he never talked about it, but when he was ill, he always remembered Mons. It went deep inside him and he never really got it out of his system. I think that's why he cared for people so much."

"He identified himself with every dying man, and in consequence he nearly killed himself," said an army doctor afterwards. "He would sit up all night with some soldier, unconscious, kept alive only by natural strength and youth, unable to see or whisper or make any sign, except, as death came closer, to grip Sheppard's hand. Sit there, just because he had promised the dying man that he would. . . ." It was while he crouched in the trenches one night during the weary retreat from Mons, that he suddenly knew what he was meant to do with the church waiting for him at home in Trafalgar Square.

Eleven people came to his induction on a foggy morning in November. They were almost lost in the enormous body of the church. To those eleven people, he told the vision which has become part of tradition:

"I saw a great church standing in the greatest square, in the greatest city of the world," he said. "And I saw what this church would be to the life of the people. There passed me, into its warm inside, hundreds and hundreds of all sorts of people, going up to the temple of their Lord, with all their difficulties, trials and sorrows. I saw it full of people, dropping in at all hours of the day and night. It was never dark, it was lighted all night and all day, and tired bits of humanity swept in. And I said to them as they passed: 'Where are you going?' And they said only one thing: 'This is our home.' It was all reverent and full of love and they never pushed me behind a pillar because I was poor."

It was an astonishing vision. Astonishing, because Dick Sheppard was a man of his time. It could well be true, as people say that it is, that he was descended from an illegitimate son of Napoleon the Great. He was an aristocrat and a little of an autocrat. He was also an actor. But he was warm and immediate and completely genuine. He was drawn to people and people were drawn to him, and there was nothing he or they could do about it. He was eager and enthusiastic—

The old parish church of St. Martin, built from materials given by parishioners, most of them workmen living in the cottages scattered in the fields off the river

Hungerford Market where the poor scavenged and the rich paraded

The last blocks of the Mortimer Wood Pavement being laid outside St. Martin's in 1842

A mid eighteenth-century engraving of the present church. Spacious and fashionable, there were no pews

and yet he was reticent. In an unnerving way he could be happy one day and sad the next, laughing and crying, sick and then well again, joking and serious. The only thing that annoyed him was when people didn't realise enough the love of God. He was neither particularly clever nor particularly holy. The institution of the Church was a mystery to him, and the more complicated machinations of it, a constant source of irritation. "But he knew Jesus, preached Jesus, and made him real," said one of his curates. "He brought God out of Heaven to earth."

"St. Martin's?" a man is reported to have said, "St. Martin's? That's where you laugh in church." A boy told to take off his cap because he was entering a church answered in astonishment, "this ain't a church. This is St. Martin's!" Dick Sheppard himself told with glee of the day a man just out of Charing Cross Hospital after an appendicitis operation came straight to a service at St. Martin's, burst his stitches laughing, and had to be taken back to hospital again.

"We take our religion too seriously," he said. "It is not adapted for argument. It is at its worst in defence. It is only when the risen Christ in us breaks through to the world that Christianity can live in tears and laughter. Christianity needs presenting not protecting."

"What with air-raids outside the church and you inside, there seems nothing but explosions," sighed an old lady.

Before long, to the intense rage of the very rich, who indignantly left the church, the doors of the high-backed rented pews were unlocked and taken off their hinges, and the little church of the Good Shepherd closed down. Dick Sheppard went round his parishioners in Bedfordbury telling them that St. Martin's was their church and he wanted them to come to it whenever they wished and sit wherever they liked.

"He put it to us," remember the old people. "He came and said St. Martin's was our church and he wanted us to feel welcome there. He said he wanted his own people from his own parish in his own church. He told the Mayfair people that they had their own churches, and St. Martin's belonged to the people of St. Martin's. He said it from the pulpit, but it didn't make any difference. They still came."

Soon the figure of the Vicar with a slight limp became well known in the streets behind the church. "We used to play cricket in the yards with a stick and a ball of newspaper," remember the men today. "Whenever he passed, he'd stop and take off his jacket and roll up his sleeves and join in."

The church doors were opened to soldiers on their way home from the Front with hours to spare at Charing Cross before a train could take them home. Night after night the church was full of men sprawled along the pews, too tired to sing or to talk or do anything but sleep.

"There was an uproar," remembers a member of the congregation. "The troops arrived in London at Charing Cross at half-past two in the morning when even the Y.M.C.A. and the cafés were closed. Dick said they must come to St. Martin's. The papers were up in arms. People thought they'd bring bugs into the church. There was an enormous row. But nothing happened—the troops went on coming, and people gradually accepted that they should come. People did accept things with Dick. He was doing what he knew was right, and in the end, they were proud of him."

And while everyone argued, a girl who only knew that St. Martin's was the soldiers' church, came to lay a bunch of flowers on the altar because her boyfriend had been killed far away, and there was nowhere else to lay them.

Then the crypt was opened and the remaining vaults cleared one by one. The dampness was dried and the darkness made bright with lights, and everyone came to shelter from the zeppelins and the shrapnel or just from the cold, and no one was turned away.

At night, wherever he had been during the evening, Dick Sheppard went down to walk through the crypt to see who was there and what he could do for them. And what he did, he did on impulse. One night, late after a party, he took a homesick girl who had quarrelled with her parents all the way home to Scotland on the night train. When a soldier fell asleep during a service, he interrupted his sermon to stop an over-zealous sidesman from waking him. When a man began smoking in church, he led him politely to the door, explaining how heavy the air would be if everyone smoked. A tramp, complaining that he wasn't allowed to hang his shirt over the front pew to dry after washing it in the crypt, learned, perhaps to his surprise, that the church was primarily a church and not a wash-house.

"Dick had a way of bringing the best out of people," say those who knew him well. "He was prepared to love everyone, the scruffy, the good, the bad, the indifferent, and to love them as they were, instead of always trying to change them."

He often told the story of an artist who could clearly remember the first occasion he deliberately turned his back on the Kingdom of God. A schoolboy home for the holidays, he was out walking alone when a small girl to whom he was a hero ran out of a cottage to give him a bunch of faded flowers. He ignored her and walked on. Later, he looked back and saw the child in tears and the flowers scattered on the road.

This story meant a lot. "It is my deepest conviction", he said, "that at least once in every twenty-four hours the offer of the Kingdom of God is still made in some perfectly simple and straightforward way to everyone. It may be only in the form of a faded bunch of flowers to be accepted with gentle courtesy, or it may be as a Cross set on a height which we must storm with infinite courage, but whatever the offer looks like, it is, I believe, a summons to us to give love the pre-eminence and to allow it to prevail. We may accept this daily offer or reject it, we may pass it by, as most often happens, not recognising it for what it is, but I am utterly convinced that the offer itself and our attitude towards it are the most important facts in human existence."

It was because of this that when the war ended, the work in the crypt went on. Street girls and overseas soldiers were given shelter, and when an evangelist criticised him for not trying to save their souls by holding continuous prayer meetings, Dick replied by inviting him to come and hold a prayer meeting himself. He came, took one look, and went away again. And in the church above the crypt, a new kind of churchgoer was beginning to fill the pews.

They came because—at a time when religion, against a background of poverty and disillusion, appeared unreal and ridiculous—Dick Sheppard was a parson whose religion was real. St. Martin's was a place that could be seen to have its feet firmly on earthy ground. Its vicar was a man who could say without a shadow of doubt that the one thing he was prepared to die at the stake for was his passionate belief in the presence of Christ at Holy Communion. And he had working with him men like Studdert-Kennedy, who could make religion as real in the immediate misery of hunger as it had been in the comfort before the war or in the hope that lay ahead during the war, by saying real things and writing real words:

> Pray! Have I prayed! When I'm worn with all my praying!
> When I've bored the blessed angels with my battery of prayer!
> It's the proper thing to say but it's only saying, saying,
> And I cannot get to Jesus for the glory of her hair.

A clergyman who believed with all his heart and yet spent nights wrestling with doubt and temptation was a new kind of clergyman. And he made sense.

Gradually Dick dispensed with formal prayers and began to use his own method of extempore prayer, but whatever he said and however he said it, the queues to hear him grew longer. He used one prayer more often than any: "Into his hand went mine, into my heart came he, and I walked in a light divine the way I had feared to see." And this was the way he lived his life. "Faith?" he said once. "I don't believe I know anything about faith. But Jesus is my God. I don't believe I have any faith except that. But I have a love for men: somewhere in me I have love. I hang onto that."

It was this faith which made him set in motion the Life and Liberty movement, to try to untie some of the red tape separating the Church from the people. It was this faith, too, thrusting aside all obstacles, which persevered when people criticised a church which could open its crypt to anyone off the streets who needed somewhere to be for the night. It persevered when Sir John Reith's suggestion that St. Martin's should be the first church to broadcast a church service on the radio was received with shocked indignation. But it was perseverance linked with such a battery of charm and enthusiasm that people were swept into doing the things they had vowed never to do, and then they were carried away with delight at their own success.

"There was something in his expression," say the ones who can still remember. "He just loved people. There used to be crowds at the church doors after a service, and he couldn't leave them. If someone put out a hand or wanted to speak, he couldn't stop them. And when he walked away you'd hear people saying 'Fancy him remembering my son's out of work. Fancy him remembering that.' Somehow you knew he understood."

If he was impatient with the Church, it was because his vision was a wide one. With an almost naïve go-getting enthusiasm, he netted famous names to write in his magazine, the *St. Martin's Review*. To Bernard Shaw's postcard, "I shall not send an article for your bloody Review, GBS," he replied, "Dear Mr. Shaw, thank you so much for your postcard which will be printed in full in the next number," and received an article by return. When his own broadcast sermons were printed in the *Review*, the sales often topped 30,000.

As unemployment grew more intense, he didn't just preach about it. He opened a hostel for the destitute and unemployed, and within five months he had found work for over sixty men. In South Wales, where unemployment was at its height, he began a work club for men laid off the mines. It lasted three years, and then the miners began to find work again and things began to ease. They forgot all about the club, and it closed down. It was the case then, as it is now, of meeting the need and responding to it. And then watching the need die away.

In the sudden flash of shell-fire that lit up the trenches where Dick Sheppard had crouched in 1914, he had seen a need for love. St. Martin's had been his response.

## CHAPTER SIX

# WITH GALLANT AND HIGH-HEARTED HAPPINESS

Standing on the steps of St. Martin's today, it is hard to imagine the complete darkness that muffled Trafalgar Square in the black-out days of the Second World War. There are too many cars, too much noise, too much light. But in the early days of 1940, it was dark like a thick fog as soon as night fell. Buildings, without their windows alight, were lost against the sky, and in the strange way that with one sense lost, the rest are momentarily blunted, there was a groping, fumbling movement as people made their way along the streets in a communal blindness. Buildings loomed up suddenly out of nothing, and a snatch of conversation or a burst of laughter sounded loud as a gong.

Then, in the silence, the distant hum of an aeroplane or a burst of gunfire. A searchlight whitening the sky or the flickering of flames in the distance. Sirens, whistles and running feet. And night after night, the endless queues to come and sleep in the safety of the crypt.

The waitresses came from the Corner House and the porters from the station. The street girls came in from Piccadilly. A party of Jews came all the way from the East End of London, and so did old Granny from Stepney. Night after night she sat straight-backed in her chair in front of the altar in the crypt. It was the most vulnerable place she could have chosen, but she was adamant. "I'm in God's house before God's altar," she would say, settling herself stiffly. "You can't be safer."

Three tiers of bunks, one on top of the other, filled the five main vaults. Tea urns and stoves and bright paint had replaced the marked brick walls, and there was the noise of back-chat and laughter and the clatter of crockery in the canteen, as people crowded in for a last cup of tea before settling down for the night. In the ceiling, grey grave-stones covered the sky-light that looked out onto the black-out blanketed darkness of the courtyard. Towards nine o'clock, the noise gradually quietened as people made their way through the dimly lighted vaults to unroll their blankets and make up their beds for the night.

In spite of the reality of war, the unity that it created gave Pat McCormick, Vicar of St. Martin's at the start of the war, a thrill every time he walked through the crypt to say a prayer before the long night began.

He didn't know why so many people came. Perhaps it was a subconscious recognition that a church held some kind of assurance beyond the cold comforts of the Underground or a lonely cellar. Perhaps it was the sense of community—that this place, with its squat brick pillars and low vaulted ceiling was temporarily home. Perhaps it was that here at least, in spite of the two policewomen at the door, no one would say, "you can't come in". So many people came from the opposite ends of London to find safety at St. Martin's, that at one time the number reached nearly 2,000. When it was cut down to 500 because of health and safety and sanitation, fingers were immediately pointed at the Piccadilly prostitutes, and a police ban was suggested.

"Half of them are more sinned against than sinning," said Pat McCormick. "They are as welcome inside my church as anyone else."

Barbara came, dead drunk because her husband had left her. A soldier came the day before being discharged from the army as unfit for service, and spent his last night in uniform separated from his bottle of methylated spirits, crying in the corner of the crypt. A mother snuggled her baby boy into a niche in the stone wall of the crypt, originally made to hold a picture or a statue, and it became his cot for so many nights that he went to sleep immediately. Rip Van Winkle came, with his long white hair flowing down his back, and the barmaid who never failed to put her hair into curlers. And at the far end of the main hall, a plain blue iridescent cross beamed in the dark.

Sometimes Pat McCormick said the Lord's Prayer, leaving those who wanted, to join in. But he was constantly aware of the Jews and the Moslems from the East End. Most nights, he used one prayer only, and there was always silence to hear it:

"Grant to us, O Lord, the royalty of inward happiness and the serenity which comes from living close to thee. Daily renew in us a sense of joy and let thy spirit dwell in our hearts, that we may bear about the infection of a good courage, and may meet all life's ills and accidents, yea, even death itself, with gallant and high-hearted happiness, giving thee thanks always for all things. . . ."

Then, for a while, a kind of quietness.

Pat McCormick's work, in every way, was the logical extension of the work Dick Sheppard had begun. When he first came to St. Martin's in 1927, he took and built upon the ever open door policy that had grown up with the First World War and the Depression. He began a relief committee whose specific job was to talk to people, to study their problems, and to give help where help was needed. With financial encouragement from the Westminster Council, he opened more vaults so that more and more people could use the church. He put the royalties of a recorded sermon towards redecorating the crypt and the crypt altar. In 1937, he became the first parson to be televised from Alexandra Palace, following King George VI's talk from Sandringham on Christmas Day, and it was on a Christmas Day, too, that the first of the Christmas parties for lonely people was held. There was food to eat and songs to sing, and, because it was televised, a man alone in London was re-united with his only relative.

When war came, the Relief Committee was turned into a Citizen's Advice Bureau, working from a little room above the church porch, and people queued up to talk about ration books and evacuation and the hopeless network of communications to try to contact relatives overseas in enemy-occupied countries.

"This padre is human, and he believes in what he is preaching," said a news report.

"He spoke the same to a beggar in the street as he would have spoken to the King," said someone who knew him well. Like Dick Sheppard, he never failed to search confidently for the inherent good in people, without shutting his eyes to the bad. "He was the perfect complement to Dick," they say now, "because he had Dick's humility and love, and the same belief that God was a friend."

It was one night in October 1940 when a bomb shattered the lock of the heavy wooden doors of the church and blew them wide open. It was the force of the same bomb that blew out the altar window, leaving a gaping hole through to the sky and the flames and the smoke and the searchlights beyond. And in the strange way of coincidence, it was that night, alone in his study, that Pat McCormick died of a heart attack. It would have pleased him, a couple of months later, at Christmas time, to see the church, entirely blacked out except for two candles burning on the altar, filled with all manner of people from all manner of places, gathered together to make their midnight Communion. They had braved halting trains and stranded buses and the dark streets to be there. In the darkness, a group of Jews who had come because they wanted to come, stood at the back of the church and watched while the faint flickering of torches led people up to the altar.

The new window was very different from the old one. A plain blue cross made from Whitefriars glass, it was deep enough to glow; pale enough to reflect the changing light of the sky beyond it. Some people regretted the loss of the old Victorian picture, others were delighted. The new window was simple and honest, and in many ways far nearer to the original plain gold cross that had dominated when Gibbs first designed the church.

It was chosen by Eric Loveday, who came to St. Martin's when Pat McCormick died; and, in a way, the choice was indicative of him. He was quiet and intense and apparently reserved. His personality didn't hit people smack between the eyes as Dick Sheppard's had done. He was a poet and an artist, and living in Trafalgar Square in the mess and debris of war, he held on to both poetry and beauty.

"I know", he said once, "that the song of a bird these mornings does more to balance the headlines of a newspaper than many sermons."

He used to draw the sting of Church Council meetings by coming in and putting a daisy and a magnifying glass on the table. "He gave them to you and asked you what you could see," remembers one of the people who knew him. "He tried to explain to you about life from looking at the beauty of a flower. It sounds soft and silly, but it wasn't like that. He was far from soft and silly." And partly for its poetry, he loved to quote St. Paul: "If I speak with the tongues of men and of angels, but have not love, I am become a sounding brass or a clanging cymbal." "The tragedy," he used to say, "is that those words are so beautiful that very few people have ever believed that they are true."

And yet, like so many reserved people, he had a kind of intimacy which could make itself felt over the radio, and as war went on, people all over the country began to feel a strange, intangible link with the church in the middle of London, soldiering on with the bombs dropping all round it, trying, through it all, to preach courage and comfort.

A man who had never set foot in London before came in off the streets to ask for help because his mother, who had never left the Highlands of Scotland, but used to listen to the wireless, had said, "If ever you are in trouble, go to St. Martin-in-the-Fields."

A Toc H padre, taken prisoner at the start of the war, heard Eric Loveday preaching about Jacob, who took his pillow of stone and made it into a memorial to remind him of a glimpse of heaven. "Last night and for many nights past, those same stars have looked down on many of us who live just like that," he said. "This is the age of the hard pillow. Here at home and over so large a part of the earth, on friends and foe, the stars look down on their loneliness and fear and anxiety. The comfort and peace of the night has gone, and we build bridges of thought and wishes across land and water to the people we love. Life is at its most real; tomorrow is no longer a certainty, possessions are a thing of the moment, and eternity is closer than we know. But there is something precious here that must never be lost or forgotten. Hard stone it may be, and as uncomfortable, but there is gold in it."

That same padre who listened and looked out at the stars, and turned back to discover that there was gold to be found even in an internment camp, was later to become Vicar of St. Martin's.

And far away on a cold, bare hillside in the Apennines towards the end of the Italian Campaign when the war was nearly over, three soldiers crouched high up in the cold darkness, while one of them bent over the wireless, trying to pick up London.

"There was no light at all," he remembers. "Clouds covered the sky, and I daren't put a light on. I twiddled about in the dark, and then suddenly I heard something. It was a service from St. Martin's. I shall never forget the sheer delight of hearing Trafalgar Square on that bleak hillside when we were feeling so miserable. It was something I can never fully explain." The three men sat without moving, listening in silence for twenty minutes. "We'd never discussed religion. It had never even been mentioned. But somehow it had a bearing on all that was happening to us. There was something to go home to, and the rest of the war seemed more tolerable." None of the three said much afterwards. One said, "I'd like to meet that bloke." But he was killed three days later.

"The least and the last and the lost"—a month after VE day, Eric Loveday preaching in St. Martin's, repeated the phrase again and again. "It is the despised, the poor, the under-privileged, the diseased, the simple, the deficient in personality—it is these who come first," he said. "It is from this that Francis Thompson devised his idea of The Hound of Heaven: the pursuing love of God to the most inaccessible places, and for the most undeserving and ungrateful people. Base your political priorities anywhere else and you will fail. The least and the last and the lost. On what else has the tradition of this place been built, but simply that here, men are wanted who are unwanted anywhere else?"

Overcome with the jubilation of peace, the sound of St. Martin's carillon clattered out over London again—a depleted, blackened, gawky, sombre, charred London. But soon rattles and paper hats gave way to ration books and unemployment queues. Almost unnoticed, jubilation merged into realisation, and hovered on the edge of disillusion. A man walking towards the river caught sight of the light above the porch of the church. It intrigued him, and he had to go and see what it was. He went inside and said afterwards that he was treated so kindly and there were flowers on the altar, and when he went out into the street again, he walked away from the river because he no longer wanted to commit suicide.

The least and the last and the lost—Trafalgar Square was their natural homing ground. It always had been, and it always would be.

The war had ended, and yet a pre-war romanticism hung on. Tramps were still individualists with brown faces and dirty boots stuffed with newspaper, sleeping in the open or trekking from doss-house to doss-house. Plain unhappiness and inadequacy hovered beneath the surface, undetected, even unsuspected. And yet when Mervyn Charles-Edwards came from a country parish in the Midlands to be Vicar of St. Martin's in 1948, his concentration on organising the welfare work of the church was in many ways prophetic.

People were no longer sleeping in the crypt—the war and the Social Services Act had stopped that. The Welfare State was gradually taking care of the problems which had previously figured on nobody's agenda. The church took two paid welfare workers onto its staff, scrapped the little room at the end of the passage in the crypt, where visitors had announced themselves through a square grid in the door, and worked, instead, from a large, light room in the offices adjoining the vicarage. There were pictures on the walls and flowers on the table and magazines to read. Links were forged and strengthened with all the official government welfare organisations, and a smattering of heart infused itself into the red tape and classification. Card index systems were started, and haphazard compassion was channelled and made more efficient, and welfare work became an acknowledged part of the work of St. Martin's on paper as well as by word of mouth. Room was given to an Alcoholics Anonymous group. Another group, Psychiatrics Anonymous, was pioneered, and a 60-year old spinster, embittered against everyone since her parents died leaving everything to her brother, bought the whole group coffee in Lyons. It was the first time she had wanted to do anything for anyone, and her doctor called it a miracle.

"We were concerned with the doubters and the seekers," says Mervyn Charles-Edwards today. "Unless you really believe that human lives are being changed and made joyful, you might as well pack up."

One day the son of a Presbyterian minister came to see him. "He had been in the Royal Air Force, and now he was working in the city. He wanted to join St. Martin's—but he wanted to make it clear that he didn't believe in God. God, he thought, was a philosophical idea made up by clergymen to make life more difficult. I asked him what he did believe in. 'I admire Jesus,' he said. 'And when I look around, the only organisation that exists to promulgate the teachings and ideas of Jesus, is the Church. So I'd like to throw in my hand and help. Will you accept me?' I said of course I would. And I bet him he would believe in God within five years, because Jesus did.

"So he came. He came to church on Sundays, and he helped with the social work. He helped especially with some of the homosexuals who were continually being blackmailed or chased by the police, and he did some very good work—but many orthodox places of worship might have found it difficult to fit him in. The minister might have been upset, or the people might have said, 'we can't have *him*. . . .' But I believed in accepting people on their own terms—and St. Martin's was able to hold him."

Each service began to be, in its own way, a small demonstration of unity. Sam Johnson, one of the first African clergymen to train, qualify and work in England and now Provost of Lagos Cathedral, was a deacon at St. Martin's. A young law student from Sierra Leone, who had failed his law examinations three times, had his digs, his keep and the fee of a crammer course paid for him by the church, and came to have his photograph taken on the steps wearing his wig and gown before going back home to his wife and children and a practice in Freetown. A play adapted from Alan Paton's *Cry the Beloved Country* was put on, and, to the embarrassment of South Africa House, several members of its secretarial staff were often seen attending services at the church opposite.

"I felt that in the middle of London, St. Martin's could demonstrate in silence what the world needs. I remember going along the rail at Family Communion: a Nigerian, then a lady in a brilliant Indian sari. Next, a man just out of prison, and then a couple who had divorced because their marriage had gone wrong, and now they were married again. All kinds of people were kneeling there together at the altar. This was the one place in central London where there was unity."

Some people objected, as people had objected years ago when the doors of the pews had been unlocked and taken off their hinges. But they were bewildered to find that no one took very much notice.

Today, down the steps below the vicarage where the kitchens and the servants' quarters used to be, a Social Service Unit is open twelve hours a day. It is manned by seventeen full-time paid workers and over 100 volunteers.

In one year, 16,000 people were interviewed.

Files hold records of everyone who has been spoken to. There are lists of accommodation, hospitals, mental welfare officers, courts, prisons and Ministry of Social Security Offices. There are links with treatment centres for drug dependants, alcoholics and people who are mentally sick. For many of the people who come, the offer of a meal or a pair of socks is the nearest thing to a relationship. For others, an hour's interview is the start of an involvement which will last for years.

Forty to sixty people call at the unit every day.

In a small room with a low vaulted ceiling, people with nowhere else to relax and feel at home come to the unit club. There is a television and a kitchen, a kettle and a cup of tea—and there are other people. A twenty-four hour openline telephone service takes calls of distress and loneliness. In one year nearly 6,000 people rang through.

Today, where the troops slept in the crypt below the church, a Sunday soup kitchen serves over 1,000 cups of soup every Sunday, and throughout the week the doors of the Undercroft have been open to young people alone and at a loss in London. Those who are ill and will accept treatment have treatment arranged for them. Some are helped to find a job or lodgings. Many are helped to go home.

In one year, nearly 7,000 young people passed through.

In the room where the blue cross gleamed above the air-raid shelterers, a Chinese church holds Cantonese services. Over 250 members come from opposite sides of London, and for many of them, Trafalgar Square is the only Tube station they have learned to recognise. In the main hall of the crypt

The portico of St. Martin's where the poor used to shelter. Designed by Sir James Gibbs, it was so much admired that the architect of the National Gallery was ordered in no way to block the view from Pall Mall

(*left*) The delicate white spire which caused great controversy when Gibbs placed it above a Greek-style pillared portico. (*below*) The vaulted crypt, now cleared and used for a variety of activities–Chinese church, soup kitchen, folk club . . .

on Sunday nights, coloured lighting throws shadows from the pillars as singers sing folk songs.

Upstairs in the vestry hall, the room with the royal coat of arms where past vicars ruled Westminster, overseas visitors meet together after matins. Later in the week, in the same room, Alcoholics Anonymous groups are held. There is one meeting for over-thirties and one for under-thirties—both are well attended.

Today, inside the church, where lords in powdered wigs and ladies with rings on their fingers sat in expensive pews to hear hour-long sermons, a folk group sings "Hallelujah! I'm gonna lay my burden down!" at Sunday afternoon folk services; and, against a background of radio pioneering history, monthly services are relayed overseas on the BBC World Service to ships and villages and mountainsides across the world. A school and a workshop in Jamaica; a plantation of trees in the Sahara desert; a leprosy settlement in Uganda, all owe if not their inception, much of their livelihood, to their links with St. Martin's. Actors and actresses attend memorial services for the famous at the church where perhaps the first link with the stage came through Nell Gwynne; and, following through the traditional fight for peace begun by Dick Sheppard and the Peace Pledge Union, a School of Non-Violence begun by a disciple of Ghandi meets regularly in the crypt and a racially mixed group of sixth formers performs a play about Martin Luther King and Malcolm X.

In North London at an international hostel run by the church, people from overseas live alongside people from England. Indians, Africans, Asiatics, Continental and English occupy the fourteen bed-sitting rooms.

In South London, people able to care for themselves but in need of occasional help and advice, live in a house of self-contained bedsitters.

In Somerset, men on the way to becoming self-supporting work on a 5-acre small-holding, planting vegetables, looking after the chickens and running the house, at the same time learning at a leisurely pace what living in a community will require of them. Some stay a few months. Some a few years.

Today, St. Martin's is no longer the dirty old church of the folk songs. Shedding the soot, the droppings and the diesel, it has emerged from a chrysalis of tarpaulin and scaffolding as white and shining as the day it was built.

"I wish they hadn't cleaned it," was one of the first comments. "It seems to lack experience."

London has an everlasting attraction for people in search of glamour and gold, but it has little glamour and gold to offer. It has the temptation of anonymity, but in the long run, anonymity is another name for loneliness. At Trafalgar Square the ways meet. The tourists and the tramps, the celebrities and the dispossessed, the successful and the incompetent, the happy and the sad. St. Martin's, awkward in its new white innocence, lacks experience only in that each face that comes through the doors is different. The story may be old and tried, but there is always a twist in it.

CHAPTER SEVEN

# PAUL

"Night-time, I feel happy," he said, "because there's no one around and you're nearer the stars. During the day I feel lonely."

He was in his middle-twenties, tall and fair, and his eyes didn't leave mine once while we talked. The words and the Irish brogue they were spoken in had a kind of poetry.

"I stood in Trafalgar Square and there were just thousands of people going round. Everyone was going somewhere, doing something, and those who were standing round were trouble. It's amazing to think that you can be on your own in London with a population of twelve million people, and the only person who talks to you is the policeman to tell you to move on.

"The last time I felt lonely was on my birthday. It was August and I was up in Phoenix Park in Dublin, sleeping out. It was my twenty-first birthday, and there were lots of old dossers sleeping around. I didn't do anything. I didn't have anything. I had ten cigarettes and a box of matches and a friend called Tommy. I told Tommy it was my birthday and then I sat up till three in the morning smoking.

"I had a home. I had a home in Ireland, but I left when I was fifteen. Things weren't very smooth at home. My second eldest brother left first. I left home next. I expect the other three will leave as soon as they can. I never felt at home there. I don't feel at home now, but I don't miss it.

"I once had a job for three years, working in the oil tankers going round the country. I was up at half-five and I wasn't in until three in the morning and I was very happy. But I had to leave when I was eighteen. After that I made a bit of money working on a farm—good hard work. I liked it. My mind was off things and the sun was shining. But I'd nowhere to go. I thought in England there'd be more room like. Some place to stay. I came over all willing to work, but as soon as I came I had no money, so I was sleeping out again. I got a cold and I was spitting up and I went to hospital. I couldn't take a job then because I'd be coughing all the time. I'm in a Salvation Army Hostel for the week now, but before that it was empty houses in the Caledonian Road or King's Cross.

"When I was young, my father used to ask me what I wanted to be. That was always the conversation at the table—what did I want to be. And I never knew. He told the list out to me, and I never had any interest in any of them. I used to go out and buy a cup of tea and sit in a corner in a café in Dublin and I'd sit there thinking all the time and watching the people going in and out. Twelve o'clock they opened and they didn't shut till six in the morning, and I just sat there for six hours and then I'd walk out and start singing. But I didn't have any answer to my problems.

"I was talking to a fellow that was very well off in there one day. He had thousands, and he said to get on in the world you have to be no good. It's true—I've found it out myself. Supposing I get two pounds today—I won't, but supposing I do. Someone touches me for two bob or half a dollar, and I give it to them. Then someone else comes along, and my two pounds goes very quick. But this fellow in the café, he'd got thousands, and if someone came up to him, he wouldn't want to know.

"I said to myself, if I work, I'd rather have a little money and stay myself than be something like that.

"But you have to have money to make friends. There was a character in Ireland—the two of us slept out together. But you can't trust people. If a person's doing well, he doesn't want to be seen talking to someone who's looking bad like. I've had two good friends in my life. Tommy let me down. The other hasn't let me down yet.

"I'd like a friend. One friend is enough—that's all you

need. A friend is everything, I suppose. A friend has feeling for you and you have feeling for him. But it's difficult talking to people who are sleeping out. People in that sort of state aren't very friendly. If you tried to be friendly, they'd make you out to be soft, and then you'd find yourself walking into trouble.

"I think there's no such thing as a friend in this world. This isn't heaven. You can't have friends—you can't have anything that's good, because this is an imperfect world. I've met people, but everything wears out after a while. Nothing lasts.

"The only time I felt really happy was when I was taking tablets. I got them off this fellow free. I was sleeping in a hay barn in Ireland. Tommy had gone away and I was alone. I had three in the morning and three at the dinner hour and three at night. I went to hospital after three weeks. I don't know what they were. I didn't bother to find out.

"In Dublin my brother used to say to me, 'Do you want to end up like these old dossers here?' He's got his own business now, his own car, his own house, and he's got himself a wife. He's got everything in life. But there's still something missing. He has no feeling for anyone. To get what he's got, he had to give up that. I'd rather have no money.

"I've had food since I've been at the hostel—before that, I had to go round and get whatever came along. And with a proper address, I can sign the labour. But lately I haven't been sleeping. I go for a good long walk up from Piccadilly. I start walking at four, and I'm back around eight in the morning. Piccadilly is my home. It's the busiest part of London. There's millions of people about, but you're just another part of the day. Everyone is part of the day, so you don't feel alone. Even on the Tube—I'll be going on the Tube, and everyone is dead. On a bus, you can look out of the window and smile at things and talk to people because it's daylight, but on the Tube, it's dead. No talking. You look across and you're looking at yourself, like a mirror, and you look sideways and you're looking straight into someone's face. Into their eyes. You have to close your eyes and doze off.

"I can see the soul of a person through their eyes—I'm thankful that I can do that. It has to do with psychiatry, and it means a lot. Eyes mean more than looks. You can see friendliness or hate in a person's eyes.

"But once you give up family life, you give up friendly life and all. Every morning I have half a crown off the gentleman at the church. I buy five Woodbines, a cup of tea and a piece of cake. But groups of people have all gone away from me. There's nothing permanent like, and my mind has gone for working. I'm too much of a drifter, and nothing lasts.

"When you don't fit in very well, you don't fit in anywhere."

CHAPTER EIGHT

# FROM THE THAMES TO SEVEN DIALS

Four thousand people live in the parish of St. Martin-in-the-Fields. Ten times as many pour in day by day to work in it. The parish boundaries stretch from Hyde Park Corner to Long Acre, from Seven Dials to the Thames embankment. They take in half Buckingham Palace, half St. James's Park and one of the two horse-guards, the offices and the shops and the one-room attic businesses. If you take a pencil, you can draw a line from point to point.

And yet how are boundaries defined? Members of the Church Council are from Barbados, Nigeria and Hong Kong as well as from central London and the suburbs. At the Parish party a couple from Bedfordbury are preceded by a footman from Buckingham Palace and followed by the Foreign Secretary and his wife. Preparations for the Christmas Fair, with its tea cosies and rompers and beads, are confounded by offers of 100 free Chinese meals and a consignment of bananas from Jamaica. Many of the people on the electoral roll of the church are from the West Indies and Africa. A letter comes from Nicaragua: "We will be more than glad if you could kind of adopt us and our little church down here. . . ."

Another comes from Dartmoor prison: "Thank you so much for the St. Martin's Review. It has some good reading in it and I like it. Things here are not so good. The snow is 4 ft. deep and deeper still on some parts of the moor. I put out some bread on the window ledge for the birds so that I always have company every morning. I will have to stop now as the lights are about to go out. . . ."

The parishioners of St. Martin's are more often than not the people who pass through. They don't join a club unless they want to. They don't have a share in the long harvest loaf cut into hundreds of pieces and shared out at the Harvest Supper. But St. Martin's is their church. It is sometimes unnerving for new curates to be asked "Got a fag, mate?" as they walk down the aisle after preaching their first sermon. It is unnerving to have a sermon, hammered out over black coffee at two o'clock in the morning, interrupted by a dissolute Irishman asking why he has been refused communion at a church nearby. But this is just the smile on the face of Trafalgar Square. Behind it is the isolation and loneliness that is found in the big cities.

"I talked to a boy of 17 who was sitting in the church one day," says one of the parish workers. "He was just coming out of a drug stupor. I said, 'Why do you do this?' And he said, 'I'm lonely, and I can't bear being lonely. This is the only way out.'

"He'd been lonely since he was 14. His father ill-treated his mother, so she left him and he took a mistress. The boy said, 'There was no room for me. They told me there was no room. They said I had to get out. I was 14, and I didn't know anyone, so I just wandered the streets. Nobody cares what happens, so there's no point. This is the only thing to do.'

"I tried to tell him that I cared very much what happened to him. But he didn't believe me. I would have liked to talk to him more, but he went, and I never saw him again. I might have got somewhere. I don't know where, but somewhere...."

In one year, a member of the church staff went to sixty hospitals. Visiting stretches from one side of London to the other and into the outer suburbs. Even within the parish, visiting is carried out strictly with no ulterior motive. A visitor calls to show friendship and to help if help is needed and wanted, not to sell a magazine or secure a covenant or extract a promise to attend church next Sunday. It can be hard at Bedfordbury, where old people living alone are frightened of the sneak thieves who knock and swindle them of a few hard-saved pounds. But there are more suicides in the rich apartments overlooking the river than there will ever be in the Buildings.

There is the Russian woman, living alone in two rooms off the embankment, cold in the winter because paraffin isn't delivered in central London, and she is too proud to accept money for coal. The all-in wrestler and the retired ferry-boat captain, the astrologer, the comedy actor, and the colourist living alone in one room off Charing Cross Road. And Gwen, living far outside the parish in a tall, blackened tenement building in the East End. The windows of her two small rooms look out onto a towering warehouse, and when she opens the door in winter, the wind whistles up the stone stairs. For years she has tried to make the best of things, but now there are mice that run across the floor and the paper is peeling off the walls. She's proud, but she's over 80 and she can't look after herself properly any more, and there doesn't seem much point.

And yet there is a point. Gwen is on St. Martin's visiting lists because she looks after Arthur who catches the number 15 bus to St. Martin's every Sunday. She promised to look after him when his mother died, and now she cooks his meals for him, and because he is rather slow, he depends on her. Without him, she says there would be nothing left to live for. If she died, Arthur says he would want to die too. Ill-assorted, manifestly undesirable, they keep each other alive, and give life some kind of meaning.

"You are continually discovering a side to people's nature that you haven't been sensitive enough to appreciate," says one of the workers. "People show you the worst side of their nature and you have to delve deeper to find the other side. Everybody has it, but sometimes you have to dig deep and they resent it, because there is part of everybody that will always be alone. There is something that may never be discovered, but trying to discover it is part of the adventure of living."

Sunday after Sunday, Jack arrives at every service with hairpins and lemon squeezers and cigarette dispensers in brown paper bags, to be given out indiscriminately in return for a smile and a glimpse of genuine gratitude; and Rose, in hospital again, has her mail taken round to her by the verger because she keeps her only possessions in a left luggage locker at Charing Cross station and never gives any address but St. Martin's. There is the constant question of how far acceptance is justified. The divisions are blurred, but they are always there: parishioners and all-comers, traditional and contemporary, clean and dirty. It can be seen when visitors arrive for Evensong and pick their way past hippies sitting on the steps. It can be seen at the annual Christmas Fair, when the smell of toilet water wafts up from behind the stalls backing on to the Undercroft to combat the smell of young people in from the streets.

There are the sudden miracles.

"I remember talking in church when the Nigerian civil war was on," says one of the clergy. "I was talking about the difficulty of praying for a place like Biafra. When I finished, a woman who had wandered in from the Square to rest her feet said she had no difficulty in praying for Biafra. She had seven foster children all from different countries. One of them was Biafran."

And there are the constant, nagging questions that are faced day after day, with no chance of agreement and no real conclusion:

"I remember Evelyn, too, a registered male, but to all intents and purposes a female. I could never think of her as a man. She went from hotel to hotel because no hostel would take her. She was persecuted by all sorts of fears. And yet when she was well and her wig was nice and she was living in her dream world, she was utterly happy. Were we simply going along with her dream world? I don't know. To me, it seemed like 'Today you will be with me in paradise.' Today was her vision. Just as far as the end of the day and no farther. She had no grasp of anything beyond the next twenty-four hours. She was happy in her twilight world, full of smiles, outgoing and considerate. If we had insisted in pulling off her wig, she would have been unhappy."

There are no precedents, no signs to say when compassion

becomes stupid, only the frightening freedom of being able to accept or reject.

One man described working at St. Martin's as trying to swim in tidal waters. Another called it a yellow fever zone with no danger notice. "I am passionately devoted to St. Martin's," he said. "And yet sometimes it makes me want to vomit. It's like home: you love it and yet there are times when you hate it. Once you go there, it becomes part of you. You can't forget it. You can't leave it behind. It gets under your skin and you can never go back without feeling strange."

And through it all, the indomitable pattern of ordinary parish life. The parish parties, the Young Wives, the Darby and Joan and the Scrub Club dusting and polishing the church on Saturday night ready for Sunday morning. Thursday Night at Eight for the young and uncommitted, the Centurions Arms for the lonely, and the Five Farthings, playing football in the floodlit courtyard at night, constantly teetering on the edge of trouble. The smell of chestnuts at Christmas time, the tree and the pictures on the Christmas cards, and Lil the cleaner arriving at seven o'clock in the morning on the 163 and working through eighteen dusters a week. The knock on the door at night-time and the agony of sending someone away until the morning, the irony of being showered with gifts by the criminal fraternity when you leave, and wondering where the gifts have come from. The endless, improbable, practical difficulties, like finding a piano for a pianist just out of prison.

"I learned what Christianity really is while I was at St. Martin's," says one priest who now has his own parish with five curates working under him. "By the time I left, I knew what I was meant to do wherever I went. When I went there, I knew I was going to be a priest. I was going to teach people about God and how to say their prayers. But while I was there, I saw what the church should be doing. It all became clear. A priest must be a person who has independence and can use it on behalf of others. You have to be determined to bring unity and understanding and encouragement. You've got to see yourself doing it, and you've got to believe that you can do it. But the whole point is that it's done in such an undramatic way."

10.30 a.m. A man walks past an old lady feeding the pigeons in the passage and up the stone stairs to the clergy offices. He is just out of Pentonville prison. His wife's sister has stolen money from her firm's till to pay the electricity and the firm hasn't found out yet. What should he do?

12.40 p.m. A pigeon sticks fast in the jelly put round the parapet of the church to deter pigeons. An angry crowd collects and threatens to call the RSPCA. A deputation steams up the stairs and rings the bell.

4.00 p.m. A boy calls. He has hitch-hiked from Blackpool with his girlfriend who tore her stockings climbing off the lorry and lifted another pair from Woolworth's. She has been taken to a magistrate's court and the case comes up in an hour. The church seemed the right place to come because she's expecting a baby.

9.15 p.m. A schizophrenic on the run from mental hospital. He isn't a voluntary patient. His mind has cleared and he is frightened to go back.

One day, ordinary in its trivia, its tragedy and its irony. The man out of prison paid back the debt week by week and the firm never knew it had been taken. The girl who stole a pair of stockings was bound over to keep the peace because the court was relieved to be able to hand her on to the church. To the intense disappointment of the crowd, the pigeon flew away; but the schizophrenic, in a strange hospital bed for the night, had no easy freedom waiting to wake him the next morning.

Jesus said make the people sit down. Inside the church, endlessly day after day, they do sit down, from nine in the morning until nine at night, the sad, the cheated and the aggressive, the unnecessary, thrown up like driftwood on the tide. Kindness is a gesture longed for, resented and rejected; bread from heaven a commodity which perversely and monotonously turns to stone. On Sunday, they sit in the soup kitchen, for the most part in an expressionless silence, the queue endlessly shuffling forward to have a soft cardboard cup refilled with a ladle of soup. "I've got rich friends, see. I could be with them. They asked me. They asked me—but I didn't choose. . . ." There is a radio and an occasional tentative effort to introduce a prayer or a hymn; the dread of overt evangelism, and the fear of not loving the Lord enough. Gratitude is unheard of, except in that men walk for miles Sunday after Sunday to be given next to nothing. It is deceptively easy to pinpoint the parish boundary, to catalogue its residents in a card index, to mark down their likes and dislikes, their prejudices and predilections, their children, their illnesses and their eccentricities. There are nine West End theatres, twelve leading clubs, hotels and cafés, restaurants, government ministries and hospitals. Since the premature unit of Charing Cross Hospital moved out of London, there are fewer heart-breaking baptisms, but people still get old and sick and die, as they do in any parish anywhere in the world. Except that here, in spite of the links that last for years and the knots that never seem to become untangled, the most evident sacrament is the sacrament of the present moment.

"I remember a boy sitting outside on the steps, and his mother in tears in the church because he wouldn't speak to her. He'd been living out, and she'd come to fetch him and take him home, and he wouldn't go."

The clergyman who remembers that moment has now left St. Martin's, but the picture remains in his mind.

"I spoke to him. He said he couldn't go home yet. There was no father, and his mother wouldn't give him any freedom. He wasn't bitter—in a way he understood her. But he wouldn't speak to her, and he wouldn't go home with her. Perhaps the next day, or the next, but not yet. Not until they'd both learned more tolerance. More acceptance.

"I don't know what happened to them. You never do. You can't force help on people. At St. Martin's it was always faces coming for a brief moment out of the faceless."

CHAPTER NINE

# THE VICAR

Austen Williams, Vicar of St. Martin-in-the-Fields since 1956, has been described as a man with grey hair and an unusual voice. It is probably the only description he would allow. "I don't like talking about myself or what I do," he says. "I'd rather get on and do it." Reading about himself he finds even more uncomfortable. "Taken out of context I sound like a fool tossing trite sayings over his shoulder." Nevertheless, biographical details are not enough.

He is neither a theologian nor an academic. Someone more clever might have turned St. Martin's into a powerhouse of politics or theology. He left school with no thought of going on to university. Sermons are hammered out after intense thought. Praying in a remotely satisfying way was only arrived at after throwing out all the intellectual books on prayer. "I can't prove what I believe," he says. "I don't believe because of the creed or the Bible or the Church. I believe because I believe." Probably the most impressive thing about him is that he believes up to the hilt. "Christ is very real to me," he says. "He leads me. I am always trying to catch up with him, and he has always arrived before ever I got there."

Christianity he calls a game of rummy. "It is not and never should be a bridge-playing clique." The Church he sees as an accepting society. A society willing to be vulnerable and open to the community around. "I wouldn't be able to go along with the Church if it didn't care about the difficult, the non-conformist, the bloody-minded. It would seem to me to be a denial of the gospel." St. Martin's he sees as a place with the freedom to let things happen, "because I am utterly convinced that God is alive and at work here today. I know because of what I have seen."

More than anything, he delights in turning a situation on its head and finding it works better that way; in throwing a hand grenade into the middle of a stalemate and watching the pieces settle back into a new pattern. "I remember wheeling a wheelbarrow upside down when I was very young," he says. "A stupid woman told me how to wheel it properly. We were living in different worlds."

The tendency to turn things upside down and to find, incredibly, that they work better that way, has never left him.

He became a priest through living at a Toc H hostel when he was working in London as a clerk, immediately after leaving school. "I enjoyed people, and I thought it might be fun." At first, it was fun. "I was a bit baffled by Church, but as a curate it's possible to get by. You learn the tricks of the trade. . . ." But at the age of 29, the only Anglican chaplain among 1,200 men in a prison camp at the start of the war, the tricks of the trade weren't enough.

"I was in prison camp four and a half years. If you were going to preach, you had to sit down with a New Testament and work the thing out. Your commentaries and shelves of books were no longer available. You had to find out exactly what you believed in. Eventually you could pretend there as well as you can pretend anywhere, but to begin with, you were stripped down a bit. There was no privacy. You couldn't go to the lavatory by yourself. You just had to learn to live with yourself and your inadequacies.

"In that situation, Christ made sense. He understood."

This, perhaps, was the gold in the hard stone that Eric Loveday had preached about in 1941.

"I was given a New Testament. I used to read right through one of the gospels, and when I'd finished, I could shut my eyes and see Christ quite clearly. For all the wretchedness of war, I don't think religion would have been real for me without it.

"That is why I accept things here at St. Martin's which might make some people say, 'For God's sake, you can't have that in the church of God'. To me, there is no alternative. For four and a half years, there was absolutely no avoidance. You couldn't contract out. The people you didn't like were always round you, and there was no evasion. You couldn't get on a bus and go to your club or the pictures or your country cottage. You couldn't get away. And gradually, because you couldn't get away from them, people became acceptable—or if not acceptable, at least you didn't throw up at them. You discovered the men who didn't fit in—the unattractive ones who smelled a bit or couldn't talk sense or were bores or unhappy or sad.

"St. Martin's is like an internment camp. There are the people who smell in some way or don't use the right language. They are a threat and a bore and a mess. But you can't exclude them. You live with. You get fed up with. And you live through getting fed up with and you just go on. There is no getting away."

"We say 'I believe in God the Father' in the creed," says one of his curates, "and the natural corollary to that is that you believe all mankind are God's children. Austen would treat the shabbiest, smelliest, dirtiest, most drunken people as though they were God's children. He wouldn't bang the door in their faces. He only bangs the door in the faces of the ones he knows will come back for more because it's all part of the game and they know he cares for them."

At the same time, he is not unrealistic. "There are a number of people at St. Martin's," he says, "who are praying and living at a greater depth than can conceivably be imagined by outsiders. They are loving at a depth which is extremely costly. Some of the work fills one with a feeling almost of nausea because there is a forsakenness about it which has to be dealt with in some way. It has to be accepted. You have to face the fact that there are a large number of people who don't grow any more attractive the nearer you get to them. Some of them become less and less attractive the nearer you

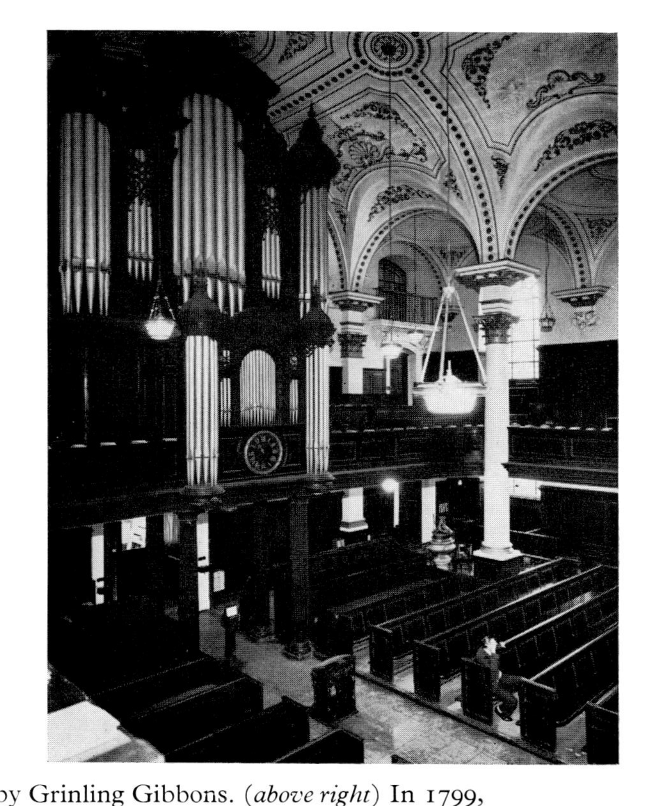

(*above left*) The high polished pulpit was carved by Grinling Gibbons. (*above right*) In 1799, the present organ replaced the one on which Handel played and caused a storm of disapproval

(*above left*) The font, in which King Charles II was baptised, was given to the old church in 1698 as a thank offering. (*above right*) St. Martin the soldier gave half his cloak to a beggar, and dreamed that the beggar was Christ—a legend on which much of the later work of the church has been built

get to them because they tend to put their dirt where they put their love, and it can be very unattractive indeed. Suffice it to say that they also fit in. I can't account for it, but they do."

St. Martin's today has become a place where it is understood that anything might happen. Praying is still extempore. Congregations accustomed to a Cook's tour of the world's trouble spots and a prayer for the Queen and country are told instead, "We don't have to tell God: he knows already. We don't have to ask him to intervene: he's there already. We have to try inventively and imaginatively to catch up with him." Identification is not so much with Paul and the prophets as with Zacchaeus the little man, Mary the sinner, Peter who kept falling down, and David, wanton and wonderful and sometimes weak. The blessing constantly used at the end of the service is indicative of the place: "And now may courage, gaiety and a quiet mind be yours. . . ." The parson may be heckled or a sidesman blasted with abuse, and the service will continue equably enough. A boy will sleep or a woman snore, and there will be no further reaction than a nudge when the snoring threatens to dominate.

"I ask a lot of my congregation. I ask that it should be extremely tolerant. As a result, a marvellously rich variety of people with twitches and all kinds of oddities come to services on Sunday. But they're all right. They fit in, and no one gets in a state about them. It is found that they aren't a danger after all.

"A man came up to me after one evening service. He said he didn't think it was important, but maybe I should know that during the intercessions a woman sitting next to him had produced a bottle of gin from her handbag and consistently drunk from it. I tried to reassure him that maybe it was a very good thing he had shared a prayer-time with such a person. Perhaps that is what St. Martin's is for. Perhaps it was a worthwhile experience for that man to have sat next to that woman. He had found that he wasn't next to a problem—'gin-drinking during prayers', 'long hair', 'nitty hair' or something. He was next to a person, totally different from anybody else. Her twitch at that moment was drinking gin. Maybe it enabled her to pray."

To believe this and to be Vicar of St. Martin's is like nuts and wine. Always a contradiction, Austen Williams has a reverence for life, and at the same time, a disconcertingly basic delight in living it. More at home with a Graham Greene novel or a book of modern poetry than with Barth or Bultmann, he likes "to enjoy sideways and incidentally". Reluctant to manipulate God or other people by pointing to situations and saying "look what God has done" he says instead, "a church should be the kind of place where compassion and concern and care are given complete freedom to leave room for the activity of God. It is this freedom and the things which result from it, which impels me on from day to day. But I can't tell when they are going to happen. And afterwards, I can't use them to illustrate anything."

Married, with a son and daughter, his family is of vast importance to him. Because he is shy, relationships with people are often either remote or intensely personal. He appears to understand temptation because he himself is prone to temptation. The fact that he has faced and dealt with weakness in himself makes him able to understand weakness in others. "Whatever it is you ask him about, he seems to have experienced it in some way himself," say the people who have gone to him in trouble and come away with a piece of unpredictable advice. "He understands not just by using imagination, but because he has apparently met and coped with something similar in his own character." It is interesting that at the time of compulsory national service, a young soldier said "the radio is always turned off when anything religious begins—unless it's Austen Williams".

Because the hundreds of letters which come in from all over the world after each monthly overseas broadcast service delight and please him, he replies to each one promptly and personally by hand—and then keeps not only the letters but the envelopes as well. Enjoyment comes from observing the pattern of words and of people. He will wait for hours with a camera to catch a picture of terns nesting on the beach, and talk for hours week after week to people who are apparently past talking to. "I would like to be streaking on ahead with the fast yachts," he said one day at a Church Council meeting. "You must be patient when you see me sailing back in the opposite direction because there is a leaking boat that's left behind and I have to go and see what's happened to it. And you must be patient when I'm a while catching you up again because when I look inside the leaking boat, there is no engine. . . ."

Satisfaction is a young man given some money to hitch-hike back home to Nigeria, writing an exuberant letter to say he has arrived. It is two budgerigars, rarely in their cage because the door is always left open. Anger is the sight of a young girl and a young boy, a brother and sister, coming off the streets into the Undercroft. "They had lived in homes since they were 2 or 3 because a couple of adults didn't give a damn, broke up a marriage and behaved ridiculously. You see what has happened to those children, absolutely at a loss in London, drugs and God knows what, and you feel a great anger that people can be so irresponsible and damaging to human life." It is also seeing a girl who came to London from Wales, had two babies by different men, and came to St. Martin's when the father of the second baby battered it. "I think if I met that man I would be angry." Sadness is "when I was called down to the Undercroft to a girl laid out on the table with nits in her hair and sores on her body and a bellyful of drugs, her face as white as a sheet. . . ."

That is why it is impossible to make pronouncements from a place like St. Martin's. "You can never generalise. There are always the times when you have to say 'not in this case'."

One of his greatest hopes for the future is to turn the empty school building next to the vicarage and clergy offices into a youth centre where young people could come for help and information, to hold conferences or give plays or discuss; but, bad at remembering the past, best at living in the present, he often finds it hard, if not wrong, to plan too far into the future. Seven years ago, Cecil King, then Chairman of the International Publishing Corporation, was looking for someone to trust with a large sum of money and a pioneering scheme in social service. "I went to Austen Williams", he says, "because he is one of the few utterly sincere religious men within the confines of the Established Church. He doesn't regard what he does for people as charity. He does it out of affection." Now the money, given under a seven-year contract and providing the main financial support of the Social Service Unit, is at an end. Contrary to popular assumption, St. Martin's is not a wealthy church, but with typical disregard, no one as yet has any idea where a similar sum is likely to come from in the future. Austen Williams is not a man to contrive. He doesn't like to dragoon or compel. He doesn't like to make things happen.

"I am not a revolutionary," he says. "I don't know that I am an agitator. I just go on and on and on steadily trying to invent, trying to create. The creative faculty", he says, "is the greatest faculty of all. We are all creative. We can all make. We are making all the time—either a tiny cell of self-defence or we are opening out to create something fresh. The most important thing about anyone is their creative love, served by imagination."

Imagination is perhaps more precious than anything. "When I pray, I start by imagining the figure of Christ. But ultimately even that disappears. There is just a reaching after and a realisation that one is in the hands of God. Christ is not the one I worship," he says. "But through him I see what I worship, and this is terribly important to me. In Christ, God takes a shape that I can understand. He is always just ahead of me, so that what I am aware of more than anything else is God at work in the world at this moment.

"I would rather be with Christ", he said once, "than with anyone else in any situation in the world."

When a silver cross was stolen from the church, "for some

reason I didn't mind. Perhaps one day we'll come down to a table and a wooden cross. The table means something: I can see Christ standing behind it." At the mention of Moses during a sermon, he will break off to remark, "I would like to have seen the burning bush." Most of all, he would like to have seen Jesus.

CHAPTER TEN

# A LINK IN THE CHAIN

"Perhaps if you could find somewhere permanent to live, it might stop you wandering."

"But I couldn't stay anywhere."

"Well then, supposing we try to deal with your drink problem instead, while you're wandering."

"But I couldn't go without drink. I'd get so depressed."

"Well perhaps you could go to a hospital who would help you to get over the depressed periods when you're not drinking?"

"I wouldn't stay."

"Well come and see me tomorrow and we'll have another talk."

In the minds of many people, St. Martin's is nothing more nor less than a welfare centre. And a welfare centre, they argue, is run better by the professionals: the psychiatrists, the trained social workers and the statutory bodies. A church is a church is a church. Because this is said, it is interesting to discover exactly how the Social Service Unit run by St. Martin's differs from the statutory organisations, how it supplements them, and how it liaises with them.

In the social field, perhaps more than in many other fields, incompetence is disastrous. St. Martin's has a reputation to fall back on, but over the last ten years, it has proved that it is not reliant on its reputation.

Immediately after the Second World War, the welfare department at St. Martin's was a single small room beneath the church at the end of a long dark passage. Visitors announced themselves through a square grill in the door. Work was carried out mainly among the destitute, supplying clothes and food: a pair of shoes or a shirt, bread and a cup of tea and money for a room for the night. In 1948 two people were taken onto the full-time staff of the church as welfare workers. Neither was trained in psychiatry or sociology. The office was moved upstairs to a room alongside the vicarage, and for the first time, welfare work became an openly acknowledged part of the church's ministry, instead of a quixotic underground adventure.

One of the workers, Eileen Sprules, had come straight from her work with MI5, with no more experience in the job she was to do than a kind heart, a sympathetic ear and a shrewd eye. "We had to recognise our own limitations," she says. "It would have been stupid to imagine we could deal single-handed with everything. We were a link in the chain. It is a great temptation to become interested in a person and to think you can do everything for them. Very often someone else is much better equipped to do the job. Knowing who to contact, where and when, was very important, and it built up relationships outside the church."

Links were made with Moral Welfare, the Family Welfare Association, the National Assistance Board and many other statutory and voluntary organisations. The London County Council, situated across the road, was willing to take habitual criminals and young innocents and put them into hostel accommodation where one would be unlikely to come across the other. Salvation Army and Church Army hostels were used, and links made with both organisations which are still strong today.

"St. Martin's had a great reputation," says Mervyn Charles-Edwards, who was vicar at that time. "We argued from strength. The work done by St. Martin's is very respected by people who don't go to church. They seem to think it is what Christianity should be about. We didn't pretend to be amateur psychiatrists. That would have been fatal. We didn't try to be superior. We acted as a background: a clearing-house to pass people on to the right quarters. And we did what we could to put a little Christian spirit into the official bodies and save them from red tape and classification."

Today, an assortment of strange, sick and sad people still keep in touch with Eileen Sprules. Many of them go to spend a few days' holiday at her Devon cottage. "The difference was that we were able to make real friends of people," she says. Men and women waited to be interviewed in an atmosphere closer to a doctor's waiting room than a doss-house hall. "I made it as much like a home as I could. I had little ornaments on my desk. Some of the down-and-out old men loved to pick up a little china tortoise. That sort of thing seemed to make them feel we cared. One man loved flowers. If I had some flowers in my room waiting to be arranged, I used to ask him to put them in water. He made them look beautiful." A West Indian tailor, grateful for help with his rent, returned months later with a present. "It was a bright blue silk coat lined with scarlet. He had made it very carefully. His eyes were shining with pleasure."

Each week began with a short time of prayer in the Dick Sheppard Chapel, down in the crypt below the church, and it still begins in that way today. "Later in the week, we had communion," remembers Eileen Sprules. "I always took all these people with me in my mind. The whole background of the welfare work was the church. It was very informal in our day, but it had to go through different stages. The time had to come when it needed someone to develop it. Each stage has been a brick in the building. Ours was a groping beginning which had to be."

The most significant expansion of the unit came in 1964, and it came from an unexpected source. Cecil King, the press lord, then Chairman of the International Publishing Corporation, read about an Australian organisation called Lifeline. "When I went to Australia", he says, "I met the man who started Lifeline. I had lived my life in the newspaper world, and I thought I had come up against every kind of problem, but the day I went there, a lorry driver came in. He had picked up three children stranded by the roadside when he was driving through the country in the early morning. They had been turned out by their parents, and he brought them to Lifeline. I didn't know that people could treat their children like pets they had grown tired of. It made a great impression on me.

"When I came back to England, I rang Austen. I said, 'Why don't you start this at St. Martin's? If I tell people to ring 109 Cheyne Walk where I live, they'll ask why. But everyone knows St. Martin's.'"

With seven years solid financial backing added to the money already brought in by a proportion of the vicar's yearly radio appeal, a full-time staff was employed in the warren of basement offices below the vicarage. They are helped by a network of nearly 100 volunteers. Open an average of twelve hours a day, an all-night telephone is manned to take emergency calls. In one year, 16,000 interviews are conducted in the six small interview rooms. For some, the constant banter of bargaining over money, the constant complaints and abuse, are necessary to life itself. For others, a friendship is begun which lasts for years. Success is keeping a man out of prison for twelve weeks, instead of ten.

Among the workers, there is neither dressing up nor dressing down to the level of clients. Judy answers the door in a silk cat-suit, Heather in jeans, David in his grey office suit. There is no pretence. In an uncontrived way, barriers, rather than being broken down, are never built up. Roman Catholics, Congregationalists, Methodists and Church of England work together. Although there are those who for some time do not even realise that they are part of a church, others who are Christian take communion together, whatever their denomination. There are no trained social workers. One man was a banker, another an accountant, another was in forestry. One man who is a solicitor provides constantly required legal advice. All were dissatisfied with the lives they were living, and since payment is low and lacks the security of a pension, life now must presumably be well worthwhile.

The present Director of the unit, Norman Ingram-Smith, came to St. Martin's from St. Luke's Alcoholic Rehabilitation Centre in South London, where he had been working as warden. A Congregationalist who nearly became a full-time minister in the Congregational Church, he finds the link between the church and the work of the unit real and valuable. Pressed for a description he calls himself a professional friend. People who see him at work call him a brilliant amateur psychiatrist. With a dislike of technical jargon, he would call reality therapy commonsense. Faced with the accusation of turning the church into a glorified welfare centre, he says, "I would rather work in a glorified welfare centre than in a spiritual scented bath. Most places are spiritual scented baths, and nothing much happens." Challenged with being a professional do-gooder, he says, "It seems to me that you can only do good or do bad. Personally I'd rather try to do good." Whether he is chairing a government committee, preaching a sermon in the church on Sunday, or talking to a tramp, he wears a well-cut suit. "I don't believe in pretending to be what I'm not." Asked to justify the existence of a church-orientated welfare centre alongside statutory organisations, he says, "People want to feel they are doing something for themselves. When you get into a humanist, state-run organisation, you are hitched onto a conveyor belt and you go flying through with very little time for discussion. There is an itch to cure rather than to care."

The value of working for a church, is freedom. "The Church gives you security. It enables you not to have to be technical. If you are working with a white coat on in a mental hospital, you've got to cure. When I was at St. Luke's Hostel, St. Martin's sent me an alcoholic who was so bad that I had to get him into hospital. Every time he came out of hospital, he was drunk before he reached the hostel. I couldn't do anything with him. In my first week here, two years later, he came in. He didn't recognise me, and after a couple of months seeing me regularly he was living in a room of his own, earning money and on the way to being well. He said 'I wish I'd met you years ago.'

"I could do nothing for him when I had an alcoholic unit and five nurses on the staff. Here, in a bumbling church set-up, it was terribly easy. Once I could do nothing for him—now he was ready for help."

There is also the value of time. Without the professional itch to cure, but only the fascination of discovering the key to an apparently inexplicable personality, there is time to build up a relationship gradually, without contriving or bulldozing. "We don't do anything here that the state wouldn't do. We just do it differently. People don't come in here trammelled with rule books. They know that we sit here free to do what we like. State organisations can probably do more for people because they have greater resources, but the people who go to them know that there are rules. It's like playing a fruit machine: if you don't get three lemons, you won't get the maximum. Here, you may get the maximum for no other reason than that the person interviewing feels led to do something. Sometimes I feel led to do nothing at all. If I was in government service, I'd have to do something. You've got rules there, and if a man can say yes to four things he gets £3. I can have a man spinning me a lovely story and I can think, 'No, I'm not going to give you anything'. And I don't."

Some problems are basically simple. "There are people who are hungry and you give them a meal and tell them how to provide the next meal for themselves." Others are deep-seated and complicated, and they take a great deal of time. "There is a boy who comes to me, and because he can't get anyone to love him, he enjoys hating. He cherishes the emotion of hate in the way the rest of us cherish the emotion of love. In time, he may turn out to be different. I have another person who suffers from aggression. I've known him for ten years. Everybody wants more time than you can give them. Some people go on coming to you for years, and it's only the promptings of God that tell you to keep on."

'Doc' Livingstone, with the latest pamphlet on squatters in Croydon or the route of next weekend's charity march, can sit and watch television in the club with the sailor whose mates tattooed L.O.V.E. on his knuckles one drunk night in a Northern port, and they can argue the toss with men and women whose backgrounds might be regarded as more conventional. Membership of the club is limited to clients with a job and the beginnings of a future. Apart from the occasional mood or flash of temper, conversation is relaxed and free, with no onus to impress. A boy going through withdrawal from drugs or struggling to stay out of prison may live at the unit for several months because his need is constant and demanding. Religion is oblique rather than overt. "I wish I could enjoy life like all of you in the office," said a boy called Peter. "You arrive in the morning and you're all happy. I never feel happy. I just put it on. But I know you all well enough and see you all long enough to know that it's real."

"I don't feel impelled to give people Christianity," says Norman Ingram-Smith. "I would rather put them in a Christian setting, and then like Peter, they will get something of God out of it."

A continual stream of people come down the steps to knock on the door of the unit throughout the day. They are indicative of the good and the evil of collective care; the strength and the cruelty of individual freedom. The idle and the feckless at first glance are many. Under closer scrutiny, they are few. The majority are people for whom life has got out of hand, because, as the Red Queen said to Alice, it takes all the running you can do to keep in the same place. There are ex-prisoners unable to find their way back into society again; men and women with all kinds of mental problems for whom life has become twisted and out of proportion; alcoholics, drug addicts, sexual deviants. There are gamblers and there are husbands and wives whose marriages have broken or floundered. There are many who are physically destitute, many more who are mentally destitute, and some who are so negative that they are little more than a blob on the horizon.

"So often when people get into difficulties they tend to flash around looking outside themselves. They see facts that have gone wrong, and they think there are facts that can be put right. But there is something inside all of us that we need to discover. Very often it is something inside that has gone wrong, and if that can be put right, the facts will follow. This, to me, is the illustration of the fact that 'My kingdom is not of this world'. People latch onto the kingdom of this world very easily, but when the kingdom of this world falls to pieces, we must look in the proper place for the proper answer that will put things right. That place is within us."

In the files stacked round the walls of the main office of the unit there are case histories, card indexes and medical notes. There is also indexed information on government and voluntary facilities. Close links are maintained with the Ministry of Social Security, the Family Welfare Association and the Citizens' Advice Bureau. Ten minutes away, the offices of the National Association of Voluntary Hostels liaise closely with the unit. Started from St. Martin's along with the Bow Street Probation Office because of the number of men pitched from pillar to post like so much matter out of place, the association has comprehensive records of the kind of accommodation available in hostels all over the country, so that it is possible to place a man where he won't immediately be turned out onto the street again. Used by almoners, probation officers and police and handling up to 5,000 placements a year, it is hoped to be able to extend the association to serve the whole of the country as it serves London.

Local and national government co-operation is increasing, and it is two-way. Students writing theses for university and college degrees come for two or three weeks to observe and criticise and learn. Norman Ingram-Smith has sat on government working parties, and both he and the vicar serve on many social services committees. "We try to serve in some capacity on the committee of every organisation or agency we use," says Norman Ingram-Smith. "Then we can state the case in principle." On the Probation After-Care Committee, he is also chairman of several committees which are off-shoots of statutory organisations. "This," he says, "is one of the times when I regret that I don't have a dog collar. It is a missed opportunity. If people think you are efficient enough to ask you to be chairman of two or three of their committees, it's a pity they are not aware that you are very much the employee of the Church."

Many of the men who arrive at the church homeless through alcoholism, mental inadequacy of some kind, or simply through age or illness, are given a ticket to take them to the Government-run Reception Centre at Camberwell in South London, an institution which can house up to 1,000 men a night. Close links are kept with the welfare officers at the centre, who are informed when anyone is coming. On arrival, men are given a bath, a meal and a bed for the night, and in the morning, like the workings of a gigantic sorting machine, they are interviewed and either sent on their way, allowed to stay with the 200 or so other men in the residential quarters of the centre, or sent directly to a hospital or clinic. With plans to develop into five smaller, more intimately run hostels spread over the Greater London area, lack of change of user permission has so far kept the centre confined within the vast, gloomy, Victorian workhouse, placed awkwardly several miles from central London.

"St. Martin's is a link between us and the homeless men in London," says a welfare officer at Camberwell. "The link has strengthened over the years as we have both become aware of what the other is doing. St. Martin's are not the amateurs—we are. We have only been doing the wide range of work we are doing now since 1966. We have had to feel our way along, and that is why one of the first people we asked to join our advisory panel was Mr. Ingram-Smith. He has helped us a great deal.

"Now the link works very well. There is a grapevine among

dossers. They tell each other about St. Martin's, and St. Martin's is a direct link between us and the young men up from the provinces and out of work, the down-and-outs, and the men on skid row. It's a very busy link, and a very valuable one."

There are also good working relations with Westminster City Council. "We go to St. Martin's for basic things like food and shelter," says a Council health worker. "We have very few charitable funds immediately available, and it is often a week before a social worker can get a grant out of City Hall. St. Martin's can give five pounds straight away. If someone comes to us in urgent need of food or accommodation, we refer them straight to St. Martin's, and if a client at St. Martin's needs a great deal of deep, intensive family case work, they might well be passed on to us. We have a constant interchange of people."

Often the benefit is psychological as well as purely practical. "Many people hate the town hall or the city hall or anything to do with authority. They dislike it because it's where the taxes come from, and the water rates, and if they are living in very bad conditions, and they are very poor, it's where the child care officer came from 'who took my children away from me' because they were badly neglected. In some cases we offer the same services as St. Martin's, but in any Welfare State there are the people who for some reason or other don't want to avail themselves of its facilities. To them it is far preferable to go to St. Martin's because they see no red tape attached."

A more unexpected link is again with the newspaper world. Anne Allen, columnist of the *Daily Mirror*, receives up to 8,000 letters a year from people in difficulties. "I can only help them", she says, "because there are people I can suggest they might talk to. Marriage Guidance Counsellors. Family planning doctors. Probation Officers. N.S.P.C.C. inspectors. Samaritans. The Red Cross. The family Welfare Association. But always there is a residue of problems that silts down through all the good and obvious channels and lies like a cry on my desk. These are the multi-difficulty letters. The ones that talk of alcoholism *and* marriage stress *and* loss of work. The ones that talk of drugs and wandering teenagers. The ones that want material help as well as spiritual or emotional. It is the writers of these letters, the hard core of insoluble distress that I ask the St. Martin's Social Service Unit to help. And they always do.

"Just one story will show the kind of thing I mean. An elderly man wrote to me full of bitterness. He and his blind wife were being driven distracted by the noise of aircraft overhead. They desperately wanted to move but they had no money, and could not find out what they needed to know about cottages in the country. They were in debt over food. They could no longer afford a radio or television licence to help pass the time. 'Official' welfare officers had called but had done nothing. My correspondent had tried to sell his Great War medals only to be told they were useless unless pinned on a waistcoat. This suggestion he had greeted somewhat cynically since all spare clothes had long since gone. Both he and his wife had lost faith in humans and in God.

"To explain all that transpired between this and their eventual settling in a little quiet cottage, with their debts paid and their faith in God restored would take too long. But it happened. Firstly because this time no one promised and failed, or talked and did nothing. This time someone was practical as well as kind. Secondly because at the first sign of help the couple found the courage and resilience to help themselves. It was only when it was all over that we learnt that the very morning I had written telling them about the unit they had planned their joint suicide."

The prayer used by Alcoholics Anonymous at their meetings in the vestry hall on a Sunday afternoon, is applicable in a much wider sense to all the work that goes on day by day in the unit: "God grant me the serenity to accept the things I cannot change, the courage to change the things I can, and the wisdom to know the difference." When a service of thanksgiving was held at St. Martin's on the twenty-

Four Vicars of St. Martins: (*top left*) Dick Sheppard, 1914–1927; (*top right*) Pat McCormick, 1927–1940; (*bottom left*) Eric Loveday, 1941–1948; (*bottom right*) Mervyn Charles-Edwards, 1948–1956

Austen Williams, Vicar of St. Martin's since 1956. "I am utterly convinced that God is alive and at work here today"

first anniversary of the founding of Alcoholics Anonymous, a stranger said, "But they aren't alcoholics—they look so ordinary and nice." "They are nice people," said a member who overheard the remark, "and they are alcoholics. It is ordinary because non-drinking alcoholics are ordinarily nice people."

A social worker came to the unit because his marriage had broken up and his career and his life were breaking up too. A nurse came, and because she was able to talk over her problems, she was able to continue nursing. The wealthy manager of a motel who was once an alcoholic came one night and brought with him the director of a shipping company whose family was being ruined through alcoholism. The warmth and fellowship experienced in the crypt at the Sunday Soup Kitchen, where men can come in from the street and be greeted by their nick-name, is not entirely different from the activities taking place in the church above.

"When you peel off the layers of the onion," says Norman Ingram-Smith, "there is no difference whatever between the rich and the poor. They are all the anxious, the lonely, the people with a low margin of tolerance. The difference is that the poor complain about 'them'—the Government and the Social Security. They say, "If I had more money . . .' or 'If I had a proper home . . .' When you are rich, you can have all these things, and you have to say 'there is something wrong with me'. The poor get angry and the rich agonise, and in a sense I am more sorry for the rich than I am for the poor."

Around his private bed-sitting room above the unit there is evidence of a great deal of gratitude, and the people who come to it—because being a professional friend is a twenty-four-hour a day job—can usually find something familiar, something which is significant only to them.

"That picture was a gift from a man in Durham prison. The lamp was from an alcoholic, and so was the clock and the rug. The china bird was a gift, and the little elephant, and the bronze pot was a gift from the family of a sea captain.

When he was 55 he went home sober one Christmas, and his family said it was the first time they had seen him sober at Christmas for thirty years, so they sent me a present. The ash tray was a gift too. It was given to me by a recovered alcoholic, seven or eight years ago. He keeps relapsing, and each time he comes back he sees the ash tray and holds it and looks at it and I talk to him, and the sentimental link with it causes him to try again."

This personal relationship which doesn't shy away from affection or even from the suspected concept of transference —"so long as you are aware of the weaning processes"—is all part of the ethos of a welfare unit which is also Christian. "I like the idea", he says, "of a God who is love." A girl doesn't commit suicide when she has every reason to. Two repulsive-people marry and have children and love is to be found in their home. An alcoholic who comes into the unit has been living a life like hell for twenty years. "He is still living it, and if you help him, he is able to laugh. I think that is the reality of God."

That the God at work in the Social Service Unit is a God of love is as evident as it is evident that he is also at times capriciously unreasonable. Norman Ingram-Smith and the people who work with him would think it enough to say, with the hippies and the beats, "God is."

## CHAPTER ELEVEN

# A VOLUNTARY WORKER

As the home-going crowds propel themselves out of London at six o'clock in the evening, the men sitting on the steps of the church stand up and stretch and begin to make their way across the passage to the unit steps, and the voluntary workers arrive. There are nurses, solicitors, typists and clerks. There is no common denominator. Each one has been interviewed, selected, and trained. There the similarity ends.

Voluntary workers are prepared in courses which are held twice a year. Each course lasts a month. Lectures are given covering relationships, the types of disturbance which bring people to the unit, the administration of the unit, and the therapies and facilities available. Interviews are as carefully conducted as for the permanent staff, and there are always more people to be seen than existing vacancies to be filled. The search is for patient, untroubled people, with the ability to listen, the capacity to love and the humility to help without patronising. Some of them are already highly qualified. All need to have an infinite capacity for honest friendship. Above all, they must be people who feel useful in life without needing to do voluntary work to establish their use.

One worker is the General Secretary of a Roman Catholic organisation. Another is the assistant minister of the Church of Scotland in the parish. A girl sub-editor from the *Evening Standard* may find herself on duty with the 35-year-old marketing manager of Britain's largest unit trust and insurance organisation. A prospective member of parliament, it was he who tried, with analytical fascination, to explain why he bothered to come from one side of London to the other once a fortnight to spend three hours talking to people.

"I first came to St. Martin's because it seemed more relevant to life today than any of the other churches I had been to," he said. "The Social Service Unit seems to be an application of that relevance. I value it for me as a person. I lead most of my life in rather rich, power-orientated surroundings: air-conditioned offices, millions of pounds, and big decisions. It is like a see-saw: you need something to balance the other end. Working at the SSU provides that balance. If I miss it, I feel I am in danger of losing touch with the people who are much worse off than I am, and I want to get back. It is like not going to church. It is very easy not to go to church. Then you feel perhaps something is missing, and you go back to church again, and you discover what was missing.

"When you first start as a voluntary, you can spend most of your time doing a crossword if you want to. But if you're sensible, you will read the files and the case histories and talk to people. Your job is to open the door, tidy up the office, enter names in the book and look up files and make tea and generally keep the office humming over. Some people find this very hard. They feel they aren't doing anything worthwhile. They're only typing. But they are helping at one remove. A voluntary may do nothing directly for anybody, but he will absorb something of the atmosphere of the place, and it will make an impression on him that he won't forget. Things don't have to be a howling success to be worthwhile. The more voluntaries that pass through the place the better. They will be more aware and more receptive. They will know more about life. It is for them to use their experience or not.

"For me, it started when I was in the Forces. It wasn't until I became a Flight Commander in a training station that I met people who got themselves into the most fiendish messes. I vividly remember one little chap who was terribly nice but totally incompetent. He got into a mess over his wife and the rent and everything he handled. He was the first person I ever helped just by working things out for him, by writing letters to the Court and packing him off home one weekend.

"St. Martin's is very like that. In a way, that was a bridge over the years.

"I have been going to the Social Service Unit for four or five years now. I started off as an ordinary voluntary worker, and after about eighteen months, I began interviewing people. I was scared stiff, because it is very hard to start talking to someone with whom you have absolutely nothing in common. I think initially I was much more frightened than any of the people who were coming to me. But over a period of time, I learned to communicate more effectively with people, and I am learning to be at ease and to accept more. That is important.

"I come to the unit once a fortnight. That is about as little as practically possible, otherwise you forget things like the bus route to the Camberwell Reception Centre or how much a bus ticket is to the Tower Bridge Hotel, and how much the ordinary benefit is when someone is out of work, because when someone comes in looking for a bed for the night you can't just say, 'Okay, sir, I'll give you some money.' You must probe backwards and forwards a bit and make sure they are telling the truth. In my experience half are and half aren't. You must know that they can go to Social Security if they are out of work or if they have had their money stolen, and if they say they went and no one helped them, then there is something wrong with the story. It's a game of wits.

"The most difficult thing is that you have to make a judgement, and you are never quite sure what is right. You have to be very much on your guard. There can be things in you that upset the clients, or they can tread on sensitive areas in your own personality, and you must be ready to recognise this. Sometimes you realise you are feeling awkward about something, and it could make you refuse to help someone you should help. I find this very difficult. It is hard to have the right balance. You are there because you want to give, but there are some situations in which you shouldn't give, because people are trying to manipulate you. It is these things that make me feel worried about my own competence. If I don't feel someone is entirely genuine, I may give them two shillings for a meal—which is ludicrous nowadays. Probably I should be stronger and not give them anything. That is one of the lessons one has to learn, and one goes on learning all the time.

"Psychopaths are the most difficult. I always feel sorry for them. They are small, bitter people who can't love themselves or anybody else, and it is almost impossible to make any emotional contact with them at all. Sometimes you make a mistake. You think you can really do something to help. You listen at great length to the problem, and you scribble out miles of notes and you say you'll do this, that and the other, and they go out shaking your hand, full of gratitude. But you forgot to read the notes in their file before you started. You go back, and the first words you see are 'this man is a manipulative psychopath', and you're back to square one. He's been having you on, and you have fallen into the trap again.

"But there's one thing I have learned. I used to be cynical about the value of just giving someone a meal without tackling their problem at the root. They are still going to be without a meal the next night, and if they are alcoholic, they are still going to be alcoholic. Then I read an article in *New Society*. It said that in fact this is a great help to their self-esteem. It means that somebody thinks they are important enough actually to do something for them. I can see that. It makes sense. And since then I have felt much happier about the general supportive nature of the unit. It is really doing something very worthwhile, and you see people coming back terribly grateful. Women will bring in bunches of flowers at Christmas time, and men will come in and repay grants.

"There are a lot of alcoholics. Some say they remember vividly the first drink of their lives. They say it was the greatest thing, something really special. It's terrifying. There are others who just drift into it, men who drink more and more, or housewives sitting at home drinking.

"One was a man of 26. He was the chief assistant for a car

rental company and he came in and said he had a bit of a drinking problem. He had run out of money and he had cashed a cheque on the firm one Thursday night and been off on a tremendous binge. He had stayed in an expensive hotel and he'd run through twenty or thirty pounds. The thing he hadn't told the firm was that the cheque he had cashed was from a bank account which had been closed because he had been so consistently overdrawn due to drink. When he came in to me, he had already missed a day's work. He knew they would have taken all the cheques to the bank and that when he went back, the cheque would have bounced. He didn't know what to do.

"I said the only thing he could do was to make a clean breast of it to his managing director, and with help from the director of the unit, we sent a note to his firm. But he had a record of losing jobs because of his drinking, and he got the sack.

"I remember discussing this afterwards. It was clear that he was an alcoholic, although he wouldn't admit it. There was nothing we could do for him. He would just go down and down until he reached the gutter, and then when he really admitted to himself that he was an alcoholic, he might be able to climb up again. But for the moment, here he was, smartly dressed and intelligent, and there was nothing we could do to stop him going right down to the bottom. There was nothing we could do until he realised where he was and why.

"Another man was 65. He had a bad heart and he alternated between living in the streets or indoors with other wine drinkers. We often used to chat, and I became quite friendly with him. He told me how he had started drinking, and he said he wished the young ones would stop drinking because there would be nothing left in life for them either. I nearly invited him home with me for Christmas, but voluntary workers are very much discouraged from making this kind of personal link with clients. It was a good thing I didn't. Just before Christmas, he went on an enormous drinking binge. He became very violent, and I haven't seen him since. I often wonder if he is still alive. He can't do anything about his alcoholism, so he must be absolutely at the bottom, or he may have died. He always looked very ordinary. A bit shabby. A bit down and out. His clothes were frayed, and he had that indefinable smell that down and outs seem to have. He will live in hostels until they turn him out, then he'll sleep out in the open or in a park until the police move him on. He'll spend a little time in gaol, and then he'll come out and go down hill a bit more and get ill. Then he'll be taken into hospital where they'll feed him up, and he'll come out and start all over again until he either gets knocked down or dies with the meths drinkers eating boot polish.

"He seems to me to be typical of a man for whom life holds nothing.

"And there are the other people—the mentally disturbed people who rant and rave and the people who are violent. If you're not used to violence, you have to work out how you are going to cope. My approach is usually to keep my hands in my pockets. One man told me firmly that earlier in his career he had been a lightweight boxing champion. He was full of drink and feeling very aggressive. He came in for money, and he didn't get any. In the end, nothing happened, and he went off muttering. I wouldn't have enjoyed being wiped out by him.

"And you have the innocent. Two girls came in the other evening. They were up from Portsmouth to see what the big city was like. They were fresh-complexioned country girls, 16 or 17 years old, terribly young and innocent, and extremely excited because a man in Leicester Square had stopped them and said he was looking for photographic models, and would they come back tomorrow for an interview. They had come to St. Martin's because they had a job somewhere on the outskirts of London packing batteries, and they wanted somewhere to stay. I spent my time persuading them to go back home to Portsmouth and being generally discouraging about photographic modelling. I pointed out that most of these people weren't exactly what they seemed. They hadn't thought of that; it hadn't entered their heads. To them, it was just a glamorous opportunity, with no thought of a seamy side.

"Quite a few people in the area know that if anyone is in trouble, they can go to St. Martin's. The police pass a lot of foreigners on to the unit. Two Frenchmen came whose yacht was stranded in Weymouth. They had lost their sails in a rough channel crossing, come up to London for some obscure reason, and they wanted somewhere to stay the night, and money to help buy new sails. One of them had a wealthy father, so I packed them off to the Embassy and suggested that they should telephone and ask for some money.

"But occasionally you have someone coming in to see you regularly, and then you can do some casework. One man came to see me because he was near suicide. He was absolutely miserable. He would never have come near the unit otherwise, and he would never have told anyone he had come. I fixed up for him to come in once a fortnight. He was a small man, and his wife had just died. He worked as a messenger in the City, taking things to the post office. His wife had obviously been a big, hearty woman, who had taken the lead in everything. They had been living in a condemned house on the outskirts of London, and for a long time they had been trying to get new council accommodation. When she died of cancer, the bottom dropped out of his life. He didn't want to make friends. He didn't want to go to the pub. He went back to his little house with its crumbling walls and life didn't seem worth living.

"The great problem was to see anything that was nice in his life. He was 63. He was going to retire soon. He had heart trouble, his house was condemned, his wife had died, and he had very few friends. The breakthrough came when he described to me a little holiday he had spent in Skegness some while back. He had met a family from Wales there—Dad, Mum and two kids. They had noticed that he was on his own and they had asked him to come and join in, and he had refused. He explained to me that he didn't want to be obligated.

"We had a long talk about this business of being obligated. Then I think I managed to communicate to him that he was withholding pleasure from other people by not receiving from them. At the same time, I found this in some strange way helpful to me. English people are brought up to think it is wrong to take a second helping or to accept an offer. This had been deep-seated in him, and I think it was something in me, too. By tackling it with him, I tackled it in myself as well, and it helped us both.

"Later on, the family from Wales wrote to him and asked him to spend Christmas with them, and he went, and he had a lovely time. Now they have more or less adopted him, and life is a lot better.

"In some way, all these things mesh in together. I have difficult problems at my office at the moment. I may be there until half-past six trying to work out what to do because I am having to cut my department by thirty per cent. I leave there, and by seven o'clock, I'm sitting at a table in the unit, talking to someone. And yet it all fits. What I do in politics is relevant to business, and what I do in business is relevant to St. Martin's and to the Social Service Unit. Whatever it is, people are involved, and in the end, people are just people. And most of them are very ordinary.

"There is a prayer that is often used at St. Martin's: 'Lord, I am two men and one is filled with longing to serve thee utterly, and one is afraid. Have compassion upon me. Lord, I am two men and one will labour to the end, and one is weary already. Have compassion upon me. Lord, I am two men and one knows the suffering of the world, and one knows only his own. Have compassion upon me.'

That is relevant too."

CHAPTER TWELVE

# 930 1732—OPENLINE

The first caller is Fred, blind Fred from the East End. Every evening he rings through on the white Openline telephone to say goodnight. Then the long, dragging hours of darkness begin.

At eleven o'clock at night, when the voluntaries have gone home and the office is closed, one person remains behind. There is an uneasy quietness as the last of the underground trains rumble past, shaking the walls. Street lights shine down through the basement windows. The kettle boils for the last cup of tea. It has been boiling non-stop all evening, but suddenly the noise of the steam sounds loud. Outside, the church is bright and white and remote against the blue of the night sky. The area gate leading down the steps to the unit is padlocked.

There are the ordinary domestic details. Filling a hot water bottle. The sudden futility of a toothbrush and sponge bag. The room where the Openline telephone is situated has white-washed pillars and a low vaulted ceiling. It looks oddly like a Moroccan palace. Except for the footsteps that drag or click past late at night, there is silence. It is a time for realising the fantasies and miseries and small dramas that come alive when the rest of the world is sleeping. There is a strange atmosphere of drama and anticlimax, importance and triviality. Cursing over the put-u-up bed when it jams. Cursing when the telephone rings in the dark, and when, groping for it, the clock falls off the table. The sudden apprehension and knowledge of inadequacy, and then listening. "I've stolen a car and I'm drunk and the silver birch trees look like maidens in the moonlight. . . ." Drama—and anticlimax.

Back to sleep again or to reading a book, or writing a letter. What do you say if it's suicide? What do you say when they're alone and suddenly aware that tomorrow they may be tossed aside like a cigarette end and no one will know the difference. Only a stranger the other end of the telephone can say that it isn't so. And how, in all honesty, do you say it?

Summaries of each call are written up in the log book. There are the easy, practical problems.

> S.W. Magistrate's Court rang to say young boy up in court today aged 19. Sleeping rough for two weeks. In court for stealing two books. Needs accomm. tonight. Fixed okay. . . . Student phoned on behalf of girl friend in her digs with a baby boy of one year. The girl was due to appear in Marylebone Street Court at 10 a.m. tomorrow and wanted somewhere to leave her baby. Suggested that she take the baby with her and leave it with the court matron or policewoman in charge. Was most grateful.

Accepting people without applying any particular standard to them makes it easier. With your own friends, you apply standards. If they let you down, you are shattered. Here, at St. Martin's, on the other end of a telephone, if the people you talk to let you down, it doesn't upset you in the same way. You go on taking it. You learn acceptance and tolerance. It makes it easier—but is it fair? If you are not careful, talking to the inadequate as if they are adequate becomes a game.

> Pleasant dotty lady living in West Kensington because it is cheaper than St. John's Wood. Immediately sympathising for disturbing my sleep. Chatted about her son, an Oxford graduate in forestry. Just returned from Kenya and now unemployed with his wife and children in Wiltshire. Most grateful for talk. . . . Woman from call box. Rang to be cheered up about starting evening classes in landscape gardening.

You conjure up a mental picture, but they seldom come in person, so you never know. There are so many neurotic, housebound women with agoraphobia: a fear of wide open spaces. The fear of going out of their own front door to face streets and roads and people's eyes. Living, instead, in one room. Living or partly living.

All they want is someone to listen. Perhaps to understand as well, but that is of secondary importance. You don't have to say very much, least of all suggest an obvious solution. Nothing works, perhaps because they don't want it to work. Sleeplessness is its own drama, like a bad liver or a bad heart or a broken heart. It is their own, and it is a reason. It is a kind of individuality. Sometimes after an hour of it you get mad and smash the shield in pieces. But you don't know if it's right or wrong, and you hate yourself afterwards.

> Brent Samaritans referred two girls who rang from Charing Cross. Just arrived from Yorkshire without money or accomm. Said we were closed but would pass them on to emergency office. Met girl at top of steps and gave her and friend instructions to get to Gt. Guildford St. and fares there.

You can be lost, drunk or homeless between nine in the morning and four in the afternoon, and you'll be all right. After that, you are outside hours and it is nobody's job to care too much. They phone from the clubs sometimes because they can't stop drinking. They can't come to the unit—the gates are shut and they can't come in until the morning. The Emergency Office run by the Department of Health and Social Security functions after four o'clock when the other offices close. You can send them there. But sending them there is like sending them to the Reception Centre. They don't want to go.

> Woman from Kentish Town whose husband died a year ago. Wanted someone to talk to and reassurance about an after life.

Thank God they don't want to know the answers but only to ask the questions and then perhaps to answer them themselves.

> Youngish female in tears. Very depressed. Said she felt lifeless. Can't get out to come here. Can't do a thing. Husband in

> Hong Kong. Can't cope. Has children. Hung up when mother came into the room. . . . A man called Robert. Very sleepy voice. Said was ill and depressed and had tried to finish himself off. Took a long time to get any info. out of him. Said he had taken 200 Largactil and 5 Sodium Amytal. Had brain op. two months ago in hospital. No friends. Strung him along while I got police at Camberwell Green (location phone box). Police arrived while man on phone. Call ended. Police rang back later to say a PC was staying with him and they had called an ambulance.

You wonder sometimes whether it takes more courage to live or to die. They seem to have acquired a familiarity with hopelessness which comes out in clichés: "I'm at the end of my tether," "I'm going to end it all." You grow up believing that all human life is sacred, but for some people it could mean twenty more years of torture.

> George. Very drunk and very chatty. Going in for alcoholic treatment and wished to be remembered.

They vanish in a sea of conversation. That happens when you never meet people. Intense involvement for fifteen minutes, half an hour, an hour. Then nothing. They just need to talk. They're lonely, and the night lasts a long time.

> Woman in very distressed condition, probably heavily drugged as unintelligible. The operator gave me woman's number. Said no point in calling as he was holding line until police arrived. Operator had called earlier to check that we had 24 hour service for people in need.

The unfinished stories. A French girl in England for an abortion, wavering and not knowing where to go for help. A boy who smoked pot anxious because his girlfriend had taken an injection of heroin and liked it so much she was going to have some more. So much reliance on the present moment. What do you say? What do you do? You dream nightmares about being chopped into pieces and when you wake there are shadows behind the pillars like tall men, and the clock has fallen off the table again. When you are used to it, the tension eases. The humdrum horrors of other people's sleeplessness become commonplace. If you're not careful, it becomes too easy.

> Lady at Heathrow just arrived from New Zealand with nowhere to stay. Gave her hotel no. and didn't hear any more. . . . Young boy of 16. Worried as he had "forced himself" on the au pair girl yesterday and was afraid it might happen again. Needed reassurance. Said he would talk to his parents.

Some people always tell the same phantom story. This boy has different names, but always it is the au pair. You discuss it over and over, but when he rings again you still don't know. Do you allow him the release of telling the story through all over again, or do you shatter it? There seem to be two evils: illusion and disillusion. It is like a recurring day-dream, always round the full moon. Psychotic people are often worse at the full moon. Perhaps if the moon can influence tides, it can influence the mind as well. The word lunatic must mean something.

> Very anxious, excited young lady. Married with two children. Mother insane and feels she is taking after her. Has attended a mental Hospital for the last three years. Hospital told her there was nothing they could do for her. She is anxious to have treatment but does not know for what. Suggested she go home and phone tomorrow. Was calm at end of conversation.

Sometimes you try to imagine ringing a stranger in the middle of the night. Ringing the Samaritans perhaps. You would have to be very disturbed or very lonely to do it. You would have to be desperate to phone someone you don't know in the middle of the night. Everything is so twisted and out of proportion that it is easy to be impatient or to be too kind. It's so hard to look at it their way. The men who can't stay in a hostel or hold down a job for a couple of days. It's hard to understand why. There is no continuity. They build up something and then it's all knocked down again for some reason within themselves. The destructive element. It makes you angry because help seems so pointless.

> Simon. Pilled and aggressive. Wanted to know who the Scotsman was who discussed railways with him recently.

Pontius Pilate put his finger on it when he said, "What is truth?" There are never any absolutes. Right and wrong, God, love and hate—they are all relative. God is love sounds very nice, but unless you qualify it and give it your own meaning, it has no meaning at all.

> Boy called Paul. Ringing from hospital. Has been in mental hospital since 1963. Read about Openline. Very anxious to get all his troubles out as quickly as possible and in the effort fell over his words. After half an hour told him no more time available and he became quite calm and clear-headed. Very lonely and desperate for visitors. Advised contacting church in the area.

It's all time. Nothing of great moment, just time. Some people can never get anyone to give them time, so they have to get it from a stranger in the middle of the night. You're supposed to be holding out a hand of friendship, but how far does friendship go? Sometimes you wonder. You meet someone after they've phoned, and you give them a lift to within two minutes of your home, but you don't ask them in and you don't give them your address or your telephone number. You feel bad about it. Perhaps there is a time for holding back and a time for giving everything. St. Martin only gave half his cloak to the beggar. It worries the idealists, but you don't gain much by substituting one beggar for another.

> Charing Cross Hospital. Casualty department rang about old woman called May. Wanders from hospital to hospital complaining of aches and pains. No money.

Strange how different things are important to different people. Like sitting on a wooden seat in a crowded bus in

(*right*) The Archbishop of Canterbury at St. Martin's signing a declaration repudiating racialism and calling for effective race relations legislation, which was later taken to 10 Downing Street. (*below*) The first Multi-Faith Act of Witness took place at St. Martin's to celebrate Commonwealth Day 1966, and was immediately disallowed from being held in a church in future

Against the background of the altar window, the Settlers folk group sing at a Sunday afternoon folk service in the church

Pearly kings and queens parading to St. Martin's for their annual Harvest Thanksgiving service

India with your handbag on your lap crammed out with money and papers and passport. The woman opposite only has betel leaves in her bag, but she hands round her betel gum and everyone sucks it. She is of value.

> Robert. Been on Euston Station all night. Wanted to come in. Told him to come at 9.30.

Sometimes you wake up suddenly. It is still dark, and it could be night or day, with weird white light filtering through the railings onto the glass. The cleaners come at five, crashing and banging. The buses start to grind again. Daylight shines down and there are people walking along the pavement above your head. It's claustrophobic. You haven't written the letters you wanted to write. You haven't slept well. And you haven't yet begun to understand. The windows are shut and won't open, and you can't wait to get out into the air.

## CHAPTER THIRTEEN

# CALL IT A MOMENT THEN FORGET

"Those who sow the wind", warned a dour prophet of the Old Testament, "shall reap the whirlwind." In some ways it is not surprising that after years of preaching love and liberality, St. Martin's should find coming through its ever open doors the people who, misunderstanding love, could not cope with liberality.

Over the last five years, the West End has become the mecca for youngsters up from the South and down from the North, fed up with over-discipline or lack of discipline or total misunderstanding, in search of glamour and girls, money and fulfilment. In the absence of all four, the only belief to fall back on is the belief that none of them matters. The Undercroft beneath the portico of the church was first opened to young people three years ago to give them somewhere to sleep during the day other than the church or derelict buildings, and to try to help. Since then, the numbers are fewer and the situation more sick. There is less intellectualism, more incomprehension and more irretrievable wastage.

At 6.30 in the morning the all-night clubs in Soho turn out their lights and their clientele and shut their doors. London is quiet and cold. Groups of teenagers move on. Twenty-four hours is no longer divided into day and night. It is just a time for staying or a time for moving on.

They move on to Mick's or George's or Charing Cross station waiting room, big hats and baubles looking moth-eaten in the light of day. A newspaper whips across the street and a girl shivers in the chilly morning wind. On the front of the newspaper there is an advertisement for insurance. It says, "The last thing the young think about is death." Tom Gaston, one of the vergers, opens the doors of the Undercroft at 8.30. "Sometimes I feel sorry for them," he says, as the youngsters slip in one by one down the steps. "At others I feel they're so foolish and it makes me mad. I say to them, "why don't you look for a job? What are you going to do when you're my age?" And they say, 'We'll never live to be your age. We'll be dead by 25'."

If hate is the converse of the coin of love, this dead and alive world of high-living and half-living is the converse of the coin of discipline. It is a parody of the accepting society. It is a world of tea bars and toilets and visits to the doctor, the glamour of sleeping rough and joining a new club with badges saying, 'Make love not war' turned sour a long time ago. It went the same way as the crumpled Kleenex and the desultory efforts to get work as a casual in the markets or the kitchens where steam coming up through the gratings makes the pavements warm at night. It is hard to get or to do even casual work in a world of 'blues' and 'dexies' and no fixed address, athlete's foot, fleas and constipation. It is a dull-eyed world of homespun, cliché-ridden philosophies, grey with cramp and coldness. Every now and then it is relieved by a flower picked and not yet faded or forgotten; the short-lived glamour of an overdose; a real hippy from abroad with painted beads and poetry in his head, stoned and colourful and not yet sad; bananas pinched from a barrow or a melon from the market and a feast of chips bought with a tourist's dollar; a grey topper and a mangy fur coat.

One boy hitch-hiked to London from Scotland. After a week he set out to hitch back home again. "This isn't living," he said. "It isn't even existing." For many, the realisation, if it comes at all, comes too late.

Don't cry over me when I travell on
Forget me forget me when I'm gone
Call it a moment when two lives mett
Call it a moment then forget

Mis-spelt words scribbled in biro on the wall of the Undercroft by a young hippy drug addict passing through the West End. They are typical of a pseudo-sentimental toying with life and death which is for ever on the verge of becoming real. For some, it never becomes real. For others, like the wretched man in the fable of La Fontaine, death isn't as beautiful as it seemed from afar. It is messy and miserable and unremarkable, and nobody is amazed.

In one year, 7,000 young people passed through the Undercroft. Of those, 400 were found employment, 200 were found accommodation, 250 were given emergency treatment for drug overdoses, and over 200 helped to return home. Fifty runaways were traced. Run jointly by workers from St. Martin's, and Salvation Army officers, the Undercroft liaises with the Rink Club for young people run by the Salvation Army in Soho, which used to be open every week-day evening and all night Friday. Close links are maintained with the French church at Leicester Square and the German Welfare Centre and with police officers and probationers at Bow Street police station. Over the three years since the work began, people using the Undercroft have fallen roughly into six groups: vagrants in the West End area; normal young people on the road for holidays, often on their way to returning to homes and jobs; vagrant beatniks dabbling in marijuana; junkies, whose drug dependence dictates to a great extent their way of life, often forcing them to break the law to obtain drugs, and leading to general physical decay; petty criminals, members of law-breaking gangs sometimes using violence; those who are inadequate, often of subnormal intelligence, driven through isolation to a nomadic existence, often committing crimes of desperation in order to survive. For most young people on the West End streets for any length of time, drug-taking is no longer an adventure in search of kicks—it is a necessity. Drugs eliminate the need for sleep, and they are the only way in to the group for those outside.

The Undercroft acts as a clearing-house. It has been called

a place that requires spiritual plodders rather than sprinters; a treadmill that works by love. It is not only somewhere to come, to collect post and meet friends and talk with a doctor or a social-worker. It is also a place with which to identify. It is a substitute club, and because it is there every day, without condemnation or ridicule, when the crisis comes, as it always does somewhere along the line, there is the chance that a boy or a girl will come and talk over the future, instead of plunging headlong into the more devious groups dug in below the surface of the West End scene. By helping him when the crisis comes, a boy can sometimes be encouraged to look for accommodation and a job. By accepting the most confused and complicated, a certain hold, however tenuous, is kept on the people no one else has felt equipped to handle.

"We are getting to know people," says one worker from St. Martin's. "To hope to rehabilitate them all would be totally naïve. Many are so maladjusted that it would be impossible to hope for complete rehabilitation. But we are building up a relationship of trust, so that perhaps one day, through that relationship, when they give us the opportunity, we can channel them in the right direction.

"I remember a huge chap from Scotland walking into the Undercroft one day. It was summer and he had come to London looking for a job, and he had nothing to do and nowhere to stay. I sent him along to the Church Army hostel at Stepney, and we paid his board for the weekend. On Monday morning he went to the Ministry of Labour and signed on. Then he went to the Social Security for money to pay for his bed for the rest of the week. He had a job within a few days, and he came back and said, 'Thank you—I've got a job and I'm happy.' This is straightforward preventive work. A relationship was built up quickly; he wanted something and I was able to provide it. It isn't always as simple as that. It is often like walking in the dark."

Liz left home when she was 16. "I had a row with my parents," she says, "and I came down to London. I thought it would be marvellous. I had nowhere to go and I didn't know anyone, but I met up with three girls in a café in King's Cross and they said I could go and live with them. I didn't know about them then. I started going down to the Club in Soho with them and I met a Greek boy. One night he made me go home with him. When he'd had what he wanted he said, 'We need some more money—you'd better go out and get some.' I knew they'd kill me if I didn't, so that was how it started.

"I hated it. It nauseated me. But I couldn't write to my parents, it would have broken their hearts."

Now, she says, "I still hate it, but you get West End fever and you can't keep away. It becomes your life. You try everything—you take a hundred pills a day, and it's marvellous while they're working. Nothing seems to matter. Afterwards, you could kill yourself."

Jill looks younger than 18. A doctor's daughter, she ran away from home with a man, and lived with him for a fortnight in London until he turned her out. "I haven't a job," she said blankly. "I didn't need one until two weeks ago. I spent the last two nights at the Club, but they turn you out at half-past six. I can't go another night without sleeping. I'm so tired. I feel awful."

Peter is good-looking, with bright eyes and auburn hair. In and out of prison for petty thieving, he eats pills like chocolates, less from compulsion than for the sheer hell of it. Illegitimate, he was brought up by foster parents in Wales. "I'd been in nick a couple of times back home. It was a small town where everyone knew everyone else, and they all knew me and where I'd been, so I thought I'd make a clean break and come to London. I was 19. I'd just got off the train, and I was standing on the station, and this woman picked me up. She introduced me to the drug scene and I met another woman. I moved in with her and she gave me heroin, cocaine and morphine. It was my first fix."

That is how it begins. Notes taken from the casebook soon after the Undercroft opened indicate the flexibility of the work that is carried on there.

B.I. Mother died 10 years ago. Doesn't get along with father. Wants to go into Merchant Navy but father against this as relatives died at sea. Been on the road last two years. Left school four years ago. Hope to get into family set-up as he doesn't like hostels and I feel he could be helped.

H.E. 18. Missing person. Just over five foot, long dark hair, slim. Left home after arguing with father. Musical. Afraid of father.

C.R. Charing Cross Drug Unit agreed C should get out of London. She should be completely off next week, and mother is over here at the moment which helps. C can't stand father, so feel it best to explore possibility of C living elsewhere in Ireland when mother returns to Dublin.

A.S. Parents unable to have him back. Took news pretty badly. Eventually got him to agree to go to Church Army at Fulham. Gave him voucher for full board for three nights to cover week-end, also 2 x 1s. 3d. and 2 x 5d. to get him there and back. Left in quiet, grateful manner.

G.J. Said he was over here for a month then would meet German friend in Paris. Couldn't return yet but wanted to stay here although he only has £1. Given address of French Consulate.

K.H. Saw me yesterday and today. Thinking of getting job and accommodation. Given money for chips.

M.J. Bow Street phoned to say had a gypsy girl up this morning for drunkenness. From Scotland and was to return tonight. Trying to contact sister to see if they could go together.

K.H. Decided to get accommodation fixed before looking for a job. Church Army Star Road. Given letter and sent off with escort.

T.T. 1 p.m. Just in from Newcastle—arrived 12 noon. Has come down looking for work with knowledge of parents he says. Has bundle of possessions. Arranged for him to go to Star Road.

Today, two years later, the stories are more involved, and the effects more far-reaching. A Salvation Army doctor treating patients once a week, was allowed, after some persistence, to prescribe on the National Health. He deals with drug dependence; psychiatric disorders—depression, schizophrenia and mental subnormality; skin diseases and infections—scabies, impetigo and vermin; venereal diseases and gastrointestinal disorders.

Little actual treatment is undertaken in the primitive rooms of the crypt. Instead, it is carried out through prescription and referral. "Many of the physical disorders", he says, "result directly or indirectly from the patient's way of living: no fixed abode; sleeping out in exposed places; lack of adequate diet—in some cases grossly deficient to the point of starvation or causing early signs of malnutrition; poor hygiene, when washing facilities are almost impossible to obtain without real effort and self-respect is all too frequently lost. Promiscuity is prevalent, resulting in repeated abortions, completed pregnancies without proper ante-natal care—often with none at all—and venereal infection." Where they are willing, patients are referred to clinics, hospital consultants and specialists, and hospital psychiatrists.

Of eleven cases of epilepsy, almost all have been inadequately controlled because of irregular treatment, and the patients are so isolated and de-socialised, so accustomed to the drifting way of life, that even with the help of the Disablement Resettlement Officer, it has been hard to make any headway.

Because there are often youngsters on the missing persons list, and runaways from Borstal, reporters and news cameras have always been banned from the Undercroft. Questions of moral obligation to a client's trust or to the police are often hard to resolve. Until he disappeared from the scene a year ago, self-styled original hippy, Manchester Johnny, given a photograph by parents come down to London at their wit's end to find a son or daughter, could usually be relied upon to produce the runaway. Very small and very brown, with a beard and a moustache and a sleeveless fur coat turned inside out, he reckoned, "If their parents care enough to come down and get them, they ought to be damn grateful and go back home."

But for the most part, love is something weak, and it is something that must always be paid for. Of a recent survey,

35 per cent of the young people passing through the Undercroft said they had no friends at home; 28 per cent said their ambition was to get married; 7 per cent said their ambition was to be happy. Many are young. A few are very hard. The majority have a family and a home and an unacknowledged fear of going back. Having escaped one routine, they are caught in another which is not so easy to escape from.

And yet even here, where the longing for approval is discredited as much as materialism and the quest for status, there are the moments of truth. A painting of the church. A carefully sketched cartoon. A poem scribbled on a piece of paper and handed to one of the clergy. Elaborate and introverted, it demands some kind of recognition, even if it is only through criticism.

One boy wrote an essay. "I am a junkie," it begins. "A fix is the climax of my existence. I am registered on heroin, cocaine and a stimulant called Ritalin. The amount I get is not sufficient for my needs and I suffer as a result." It ends: "The body is a vehicle. It is an instrument which is designed to carry around one's soul. Let it take you places and see things of beauty. Make full use of your senses to enjoy things to the full. The mind must be filled with pleasant memories, not empty thoughts, naked and ugly. Everything should be seized upon and enjoyed. If you are handed something you should feel it, turn it over and examine it. Make the most of the time allocated to you on this earth. . . ."

Of the 7 per cent who long to be happy, it is hard to know whether the longing is hedonistic, or just wistful. It is equally hard to define the role and the value of the Undercroft. It is hardest of all to know how long the need for it will last.

CHAPTER FOURTEEN

# A HOUSE IN THE COUNTRY

Before he went to the Labour Exchange, Norman had planted a poppy. It looked out of place, even out of season, because it was only May. But there it was like scarlet velvet, and everyone came to admire it.

At the Exchange, they asked, as usual, what was wrong with the other jobs. Then they suggested one of the local factories, and Norman was very pleased. He wouldn't keep the job. He might not even start it. But he had been through the motions, and there was no need to admit anything. And in the meantime, the poppy was very important, and everyone kept looking at it.

Martyn Ellis is Warden of the House of St. Martin in Somerset. "I would like to think of this as a place that holds a possibility of life," he says. "I would like to see it encouraging people to reach the maximum potential they can. For some, this means a job and a way of life. For others, it means living here, but with some kind of respect and dignity."

The House of St. Martin is a 5-acre small-holding at the foot of the Quantocks. There are eighteen residents who live together as a community, running the house, looking after the chickens and the rabbits, and farming the fields of fruit and vegetables. Surplus produce is taken to Taunton market and sold, and links are being strengthened between the house and the people who live around it.

To give one label to all eighteen residents would tax any psychiatrist. Psychopath would be a careless shrug-off. More precisely, they are men who have been drug addicts or alcoholic, men with criminal traits or moral deficiencies, men with a tendency towards vagrancy or sexual perversion.

They are put in touch with the house not only directly through St. Martin's, but through doctors and psychiatrists, welfare workers and probation officers, statutory and voluntary organisations. There are no qualifications except an incomplete kind of hopelessness. For one reason or another, often with the best will in the world, sometimes with no will at all, they have been unable to survive in society. Here, they can learn at a slow pace what living with other people requires of them. After a year or two, many are able to leave and settle down in a home and a job of their own. Some have been able to find work in London, and live for a while at a house of bed-sitters run by St. Martin's in South London. Others find work near Taunton and keep in close touch with the house. Some may never move on. They are the people like John, the brother of a grammar school headmaster. Sent to Taunton from the S.O.S. Hostel at Camden and classed as grossly inadequate, he is now incapable of holding even his old job as a road-sweeper. Unable to look after himself properly or to grasp his own situation, quite unaware that there is probably no other hostel in the country that would accept responsibility for him, he is gradually finding a little of life and happiness.

"I would like to see this as a place where people with no hope, and no apparent reason for hope, can come and find hope," says Martyn Ellis. "It's difficult to see things as they see them but I think most men who come here have no sense of identity and only a very slender hold on their own self-esteem. They need stability. They have lost their self-respect, and the smallest routine practical things can encourage them to see that they are still human beings with all the advantages and disadvantages that brings. There is a role for them to play, however limited or simple. Nothing is expected of them. They are able to find their own thing and do it and make a life for themselves."

In the carpenter's shed in the garden, Theo makes a filing cabinet and a record cupboard. He has taught himself, and all the tools are clean and polished, hanging in rows on the wall.

He came to England from East Africa when his marriage broke up. "I think I was the coldest and the loneliest man in England," he says. He has grey hair and a wide forehead, perceptive eyes and a slow, kind smile. At one time he must have been attractive, but he talks little about the past. An alcoholic, for a long time drink was the only comfort from loneliness, until Camberwell Reception Centre referred him to Taunton. Now, when he feels depressed, instead of withdrawing into himself, he comes and works in the woodshop. "I've always been good at making things," he says, concentrating on polishing a piece of wood. "I never felt happy sitting at a desk."

Jim looks after the chickens. "It's like a farmer with his pigs," he says. "They get to know you. You form an attachment. They're like people: they know if you care about them. They won't lay eggs if anyone else feeds them." Jim is in his fifties. When he was a boy, living with his parents in a Northern steel works community, he dreamed of becoming a great footballer. Then he had an accident and spent two years in hospital. "Sometimes I think we're like puppets on a string," he says. Since then, he has spent his time in and out of prison, drinking too much.

"I probably had a chip on my shoulder. When I look back, perhaps I wasn't entitled to that chip. But up there, you work hard and play hard and drink hard, and when I drink, I do stupid things, and then I've got to get money for more drink. After a while I thought nobody was any good."

Jim was sent to Taunton by an Exeter prison officer. He has been out of prison and away from drinking for nearly a year. "You see Martyn and some of the others here," he says, "they're right, so why can't I be right? They don't abuse themselves through drinking. You learn a lesson from people.

"I suppose we've all got the same problem here: nothing left in life. But you're always wrong. Whether you expect Buckingham Palace or a back room in a shanty town, you're always wrong. It's people that count. When I came here I thought I'd find people were all no good again. It took me a while to understand."

Charlie is 40. When he was 15, he was certified as mentally subnormal and sent to a special school. When he was 19, he ran away. Until he came to Taunton last year, he had only spent two weeks outside prison, and because prison life was all he could cope with, it was impossible to sit down and hold a conversation with him. He insisted on taking five hot baths a day, and his skin was red and blotchy. "If I don't keep clean," he explained, "the grease will show on my skin and the police will get me."

A psychiatrist wanted him to go into hospital, but for some reason, Charlie didn't want to leave. Surrounded by the same people day after day, uncommitted to conversation and yet part of it if he wanted to be, he began to help around the house, giving a hand in the kitchen, feeding the cat, dusting the furniture. Now he will often join in a conversation or crack a joke. Incapable of examining the thing at any deeper level, he says "I like it here. I'm happy."

"All human beings go through the same processes to get to know each other," says Martyn Ellis. "These people are not so well equipped as others. The first thing you learn here is that deep down, we are all much the same. You have to know yourself pretty well. You have to watch yourself and find out why you can tolerate one person and not another. One of the hardest things is to assess how much your own personality affects other people."

Martyn Ellis is in his late twenties. He comes from the East End of London, and he has no qualifications, either in social work or in agriculture. "I didn't even know how sprouts grow," he says. Working as a clerk with Islington Council, he wanted to do some kind of social work. In a very short time after answering an advertisement for a worker in the Social Service Unit at St. Martin's, he found himself isolated on the outskirts of Taunton running the House of St. Martin.

"I knew none of the practical things," he says. "I didn't know that a person in prison is only allowed to write a certain number of letters, or that most alcoholic hostels work on the basis of one drink and you're out. I didn't know about supplementary allowances, or how difficult it is for a man to get clothing through social security." Working for a church, his philosophy of life, if not his doctrine, is appropriate. "If I had to give myself a name, I'd say Christian-Humanist-Idealist. But I don't like labels. The person of Christ means a lot to me. He showed us what human life could be. He challenged us by what he was and did. I wouldn't put it into any formal creed. As far as I'm concerned Christ may not have existed. That isn't the important thing. What he stood for is the big part. All the possibility that there is in human life is represented in his life. He challenged human beings to try to be like that through their relationships with other people.

"That has a bearing on this place. More than anything else, I want to reach the potential in my own life, and I can't help feeling that this is inevitably bound up with helping other people reach their potential. We are involved with each other, whether we like it or not. It seems to me that everything I do or say affects other people infinitely—infinitely in the sense of an endless chain of actions, thoughts, sayings and feelings, and infinitely in the sense of every smallest thing adding to the whole balance of thought which makes up the world."

A great deal depends on learning to live with people who are difficult to live with. Sometimes it can seem an endless, pointless, and rather useless business. An argument over the chicken wire can affect the smooth running of the house for days. One man too far below the mental average of the others can put an almost uncontrollable strain on an already taut balance. But there are the fields and the open country to help release the vacuum. Some men coming down from the town find the peace and vastness of the countryside unbearable. Others, like Tom, a young drug addict, find a therapeutic value, if no actual pleasure, in planting seeds and watching a flower grow.

Each resident is eligible for a supplementary benefit through the Ministry of Social Security. They receive £5 a week for board and lodging, and 26s. a week pocket money. Those who are working pay £5 from their wages. Rent money goes into the house funds, and St. Martin's supplements that fund wherever necessary. Because it costs nearly £10 to keep a man at the house for a week, the fund is subsidised at a rate of nearly £100 a week. As well as a Warden, there is a Deputy Warden and a full-time cook-housekeeper. Profits made from the fruit and vegetables grown in the garden are put towards the funds, and men feel they are doing something useful and valuable towards the upkeep of the House. Soon an extension will be built to provide a dining room and eight single bedrooms, releasing two of the old bedrooms for use as a guest room and a second sitting room. The first set of plans was turned down because the building looked like the inside of Pentonville prison. The new scheme is simple and practical. In the meantime, there are caravans in the grounds and a prefabricated dining room built onto the back of the house. In one way, the caravans have a value of their own because they have an air of independence and individuality.

Bob lives in one of them. Half Maltese, he arrived on the doorstep one morning with the name and address of the house on a scrap of paper. He had walked from Bristol prison. He had his £4 discharge money still untouched in his pocket—he hadn't bothered to spend it on lodgings, because he knew he couldn't manage on his own. Totally disorganised, roaming for miles round the country, he had been in and out of prison for stealing a bottle of milk or a meat pie. Worried in case he was homosexual, embarrassed because of his accent, for the first few months, his only way out of a difficult situation was still to walk. He walked to Cornwall where his parents live, and he walked to his aunt in Birmingham. In Birmingham, he took a job in a factory for a fortnight, walked out one lunchtime, and didn't go back.

He has been at Taunton for a year now. He has held a job

as a groundsman at a local school for a year. Brown-eyed and brown-faced, he likes working hard, and when he felt depressed and wanted to give up the job, his employers persuaded him to stay. When winter came, he had a struggle because winter was the time for roaming round. Staying in one place for the winter built up a sense of belonging, and in the spring, he asked if he could paint his caravan because it seemed like home and he wanted to be proud of it. The edges of the windows inside are pale blue and white, painted perfectly without a speck of white on the blue. Round his bed are pen and ink sketches copied from record sleeves and the dust jackets of books. "I wish I didn't always have to copy," he says. "But I can't do anything else." Nevertheless, the sketches are meticulous and detailed and very good, and when people ask to buy them, he is pleased.

"There are some people who walk out time after time," says Martyn Ellis. "I can only remember one man who walked out after a week and never came back. He was alcoholic, and he said it didn't matter where he was or what he was doing or what happened to him. But one man has been here fifteen times. Sometimes he leaves of his own accord, and sometimes we have to ask him to leave, but even in two weeks, an impact may have been made, and after a while drifting around, he will come back and have another try. Over the years, a relationship can be built up. It may take many years, and it may never be really successful, but if a man comes back, he is admitting he was wrong, and it takes courage to do that. He is admitting that he needs the support of the house."

It is hard to create a community out in the countryside with a group of men who are each in need of specialised treatment or care. But, once it is underway, community life has a therapeutic value of its own. It makes an argument for more hostels and smaller hostels. A day can be like a volcanic explosion or peaceful as a dovecote, but it has in it somewhere the unconscious value of people getting to know each other, reacting to each other, learning that they need each other, being forced to look outside themselves and accept the irritations and the pleasures of being with someone else.

There is a sense of belonging, and there is the new found safety net of security. And when Norman doesn't go in to work after all and his pipe-dream fails, the poppy will still be there, alive and red and very real.

CHAPTER FIFTEEN

# TOM

Tom is sharp-featured, with dark eyes and dark hair. If he was more healthy and his eyes less troubled, he would be good-looking. He has been off drugs for a year. Brought up in homes, he first saw a family when he was 22. "There was a brother and a sister, and they were laughing. I'd never realised what it was like. I felt out of place." He has been at the House of St. Martin for three years, and spends most of his time in the greenhouse, where he has seeds planted in rows in wooden boxes. He touches them with authority, in the same way a bird-lover handles birds. After years of not trusting and shuffling responsibility, years of being analysed, he analyses himself automatically, unremarkably.

"The plants are just something to do," he says. "I don't enjoy planting them, I do it to convince myself that I'm not as useless and helpless as I'm made out to be. And I do it to prove to myself that I can do it. I like flowers because of their beauty. Beauty deserves to be admired.

"Everyone should do something creative: something with their hands. They should make tables or chairs or plant seeds. But all anyone wants is quantity. There's no point in sitting down and making a chair. They wouldn't want it.

"A person's given a mind, and he ought to be allowed to use it. I was frightened when it was suggested I should come here—I thought it would be the same as all the other places. But this isn't just another home. You can use your own mind here.

"I've been in homes all my life. I was illegitimate, and I never knew my father or my mother. I just had to take what I was given, with no say in the matter. I left at 18—they get you digs and clothing and that's it. They leave you then. If anything goes wrong, you've no one.

"I spent a while at a farm training school, but I didn't want to do it. I've never been able to do anything I wanted to do. I've had to do what I've been told to do, so I've never really been interested. I don't even remember going to school except that I couldn't read or write properly when I left.

"I took different jobs, but it was like being lost in the jungle. I was only out of the home for a year when I got done for trouble at my lodgings. There was some money missing. I had all my things stolen, but they didn't take any notice of that. I was a bit wilder then, I suppose. I got three years Borstal, and when I came out of Borstal, the after-care people sent me to a steel factory at Stepney in the East End of London.

"I sang with a group while I was there. It was blues beat and sentimental music, and we sang in a pub down Brick Lane. I enjoyed that. The old people used to get up and try to twist, and it was marvellous. When I sang a song, I sang it from the heart. I put everything into it, especially if I'd had a smoke. I was really carried away. I used to stand in front of the mike with tears pouring out of my eyes, and people enjoyed it. It was terrific. You know yourself. You know you are nothing. You know you have nothing—and yet you're able to give something to other people.

"But away from there, I was useless out in society on my own. Finding somewhere to live and feeding myself seemed such big problems that I didn't really want to live.

"That was when I started on drugs. It was to do with this girl. I'd never been a chap for the girls. I kept myself to myself because of the way I am. I've always had this since a time at the home, and I've had to live with it. I accept what I am. But this girl was very interested in me, and she was taking drugs, and she doped my tea. I never looked back after that. I was on drugs all the time. As soon as they wore off, I felt as if the ceiling was coming down on top of me, and I had to get some more. I knew certain people by then, and I was always able to get them. I used to go round on my own because I didn't trust people. You couldn't afford to trust people when you were mixed up with a thing like that. One bad word and you could land up having your throat cut. I just let them get on with it. So long as I got my supply I wasn't interested in where it came from.

"I got quite well known. I've always been withdrawn because I've never had faith in anybody. Whenever I trusted anyone, they let me down, so I stopped trusting. I'd always had to defend myself and put up a barrier in front of me. But drugs helped me to cope with myself and with life. When I was on drugs, I was able to mix with people more. I thought I was popular.

"But those people weren't friends. They are nobody's friends. You're better off alone. They only want a few shillings off you so that they can give you the drugs in exchange. They'll put school-children on drugs and not care a damn so long as they make their £100 a week.

"It was all right when I was taking five a day. I felt confident. I felt more myself than I had ever felt before. But by the time I was taking 40 a day, I was walking round the streets like a zombie. I was taking more and more because I was worried and I didn't know where my next sleep or my next meal was coming from. So I didn't go to sleep. The drugs were mounting up, and you don't get tired on drugs. I went for seven weeks without sleeping—I just sat in cafés.

"Anyone who takes drugs is running away from something. He's running away from himself and the problems he can't cope with. If it wasn't for this place, I'd probably be dead from drugs.

"Helen told me about St. Martin's. She's a social worker—she works with children, and she's known me a long time. I think she knew I was on my own, and when I landed in prison, she started writing to me. I was still on drugs when I came out, but she made me come to St. Martin's. I spoke to

Mr. Ingram-Smith. I'd been on the tablets very bad, and I was down to eight stone, and every time I went down to see him, he said, 'have something to eat'. I'd gone for days without anything to eat, and it seemed very kind. He suggested I came here.

"Coming here has given me somewhere to live and things to do, and a certain amount of security. I've got a caravan to live in, and nobody runs round after me all day. This is my home. It's the only home I know, and the only life I know.

"I'm still not myself. I can't be, without drugs. It's more like when I was living in the homes—I conceal a lot. Once a person has been destroyed inside himself it takes years to put the pieces together again. The damage has been done and you can't put it right, and yet you've got to live with it for the rest of your life.

"When I first left the home, I wanted to find out about my parents. There was a record of my mother and my father, where I was born and when I was handed over to the home. I went and looked it up under my name. There were various things telling me my mother used to go round with different men, and that she was dead. The man there made it look worse that it was, and he said, 'Why don't you let the dead rest?' But I wanted to know the truth. I wanted to know everything, whether it was good or bad. Every child is entitled to that, even if he's never known his parents, he's entitled to have parents. There must have been parents in the first place or he wouldn't exist. Whatever she'd done, it didn't alter the fact that she was still my mother. It's a bond. There's a certain amount of love there, deep down inside—I just wanted to find out.

"I've never really known my identity. Since I've been here, I've accepted a lot. I've learned that if you aren't honest with yourself, you can't be honest with anyone else. Here, I'm beginning to try to find an identity.

"I suppose sometimes they think I'm a miserable, moaning old fool, but I can't communicate with people. I can see this. I don't want to get involved. But I've always liked helping people, so I help the chaps here, and we get on quite well.

"They can give you a place to live, a place to sleep, food and a little bit of money, but it's up to you to learn to live with yourself and accept yourself for what you are. No one else can do that for you."

CHAPTER SIXTEEN

# CHRISTMAS

A week before Christmas, with carols and candles, the crib is blessed in Trafalgar Square. Above the white sculpted figures are the words "The Lord was made flesh and dwelt among us." Surrounded by an outpouring of affluent goodwill, the faces are untroubled and unmoved.

Strangers slip into the church to join in singing carols, and men in the Reception Centre carve wooden rocking horses and sell them to parents for their children to ride on.

The best doll from the tree by the chancel steps goes to a child of 12 who is mentally retarded. After spending her life helping to look after five younger brothers and sisters, her Christmas is suddenly overcome with the joy of having a baby that belongs to her and to no one else.

Mail sacks full of stamps and postal orders from old age pensioners, housewives and businessmen begin to arrive at 5 St. Martin's Place after the annual radio appeal for people in need throughout the country, and May, who sleeps under the *Evening Standard* shelter goes off protesting and grumbling to spend the holiday in a hostel.

Christmas Day is the quietest day of the year. The streets are empty and the wind whistles across the square, lifting a stray newspaper. There are apples and oranges, cigarettes and mince pies piled on a trestle in the doorway of Number Five, and puddings steaming like a turkish bath in the crypt kitchen. Five parties go on at once in the crypt and in the vicarage for the people with nowhere to go or no one to be with and there is the pleasure of being greeted at someone else's front door; of sitting in their chairs and drinking out of their cups.

In the church at the evening service, shepherds worship with the wisemen, and afterwards the smell of loneliness and unacceptability lingers when the carols have ended.

For a month there have been carols every day and every night. Now, when they are required, the crib is silent and unsung. The word has been made flesh and Christmas is elsewhere.

Far away in Africa, a girl whose Christmas toy had been a piece of dried skin stretched across a broken bottle to make a drum, bashes a tambourine with a label on it saying, "Happy Christmas from St. Martin-in-the-Fields, Trafalgar Square."

CHAPTER SEVENTEEN

# THE PARISH CHURCH OF THE COMMONWEALTH

The first time the Vicar visited Sierra Leone, he took with him a list of people who had worshipped at St. Martin's. With the list in his hand, he walked down a suburban street in Freetown until he reached the right door and rang the bell. An African woman answered. For a moment, she looked at him without saying anything. Then she smiled. "Obi!" she called up the stairs to her husband. "Obi! It's the Vicar!"

It was the same in Lagos, with people stopping to shake hands in the street and remember a wedding, a christening or a farewell party. "I was in West Africa, a world away from Trafalgar Square," he said when he came home. "And yet it wasn't a world away or anything like. In the streets of Lagos, in spite of all the strangeness, I felt as much in my own parish as I do in the streets of London. Walking down the Marina I was stopped three times by Nigerians who had worshipped at St. Martin's, and it was the same in Ibadan, Ilesha, Lokoja, in Accra, Khumasi and Cape Coast, in Freetown and the little village of Regent up in the hills behind. Every walk was something like a parochial visitation." This year when he visited Jamaica, an article was headed "the Vicar of the most famous church in the world".

International involvement has grown up at St. Martin's side by side with the social work. In Central London it has been both essential and inevitable. And yet it has become much more than a mere necessity or a quirk of fate. It began, perhaps, with the first East-West parties before the war, and with the broadcast services sent out once a month on the BBC World Service to places across the world: remote mountain villages, desert huts and ships at sea. It began also with the sense of involvement which held an Intercession Service for India and Pakistan in 1950, and sent a letter to the government when the first bill controlling immigration was passed through Parliament. A sense of involvement which more recently expressed itself in a sign-in on race, and a starve-in for world poverty, and encouraged a Nigerian to write to the church during the civil war:

> The Red Cross started feeding children from one to ten years in this town two days ago. They have asked that those who have letters for overseas should bring them for post. I wish to use this opportunity to write to you and say "How do you do". I still remember that Rev. Austen Williams was our vicar in St. Martin's while I was in England. I was a regular face in the service, and the student monthly meetings. I indeed enjoyed St. Martin's.
>
> I returned to this part of the world a few months before the crisis. We are fighting a war, a real war, and the conditions are the same with all wars. It is indeed a primitive war. Kindness is an anathema to a soldier or civilian. All enemies are heartless.
>
> I ask for your prayers. I remember my happy days at St. Martin's. How I wish I were in your midst to tell you of war-time here. As I write there is a booming of mortar bombs shelling not far from here, but I am now happy because there is torrential rain on and we do not expect the air-raids. Please remember me to the good people of St. Martin's. Pray for us to survive this war.
>
> Yours sincerely,
> Alphonso Nwachukwu

It is an involvement which has a head start because Austen Williams is vice president of War on Want, and he has a fascination for travel which is only equalled by his fascination for birds in flight. He has been able to go and see, and then to come back and put into action. And yet much of the work that is done overseas stems from the work which is begun insignificantly over a tea party or a dinner table in London.

"I come to St. Martin's because the singing makes me feel

happy," says a West Indian. "I come because it's like home," says an African. There is rhythm and colour and soul, and that is good. A Barbadian left his church in West London because "they were polite to me on Sundays, but when they saw me on the buses during the week, they didn't know me". He came to a service at St. Martin's and found a friend from home leading the choir. When Sierra Leone celebrated independence, invitations were sent to the Vicar and Mrs. Williams because the High Commissioner had worshipped at St. Martin's since his student days in England. One after the other, independence services in London were arranged to take place at St. Martin's for much the same reason.

> It is as much up to you now as it is to us to make us meet you mind to mind in discussion, in argument and in ordinary conversation [said an article in *The Review* ten years ago]. Make us see—with all your persuasiveness—your reactions to working and living in a Western metropolis which, basically, is abysmally ignorant of your way of life. Trust us, when we come to St. Martin's, to do so because we wish to match our minds with—not against—your own, to meet you at the only level of understanding which can have lasting effect in a turbulent world: thought for thought.

Since then, St. Martin's has become a place where people can argue the pros *and* cons of playing sport with the South Africans; the pros *and* cons of immigration control; the pros *and* cons of overseas aid. The atmosphere is not one of blind liberalism which inevitably does the right thing sometimes for the wrong reason or for no thought-out reason at all. It is an atmosphere of people trying to live together and finding it sometimes incredibly hard; at others, incredibly easy. Many, who want to move more quickly, grow impatient.

In 1960, at the time of the Sharpeville shooting, when police were on guard outside South Africa House opposite the church, a white member of the embassy staff walked past the demonstrators every day to lunch at St. Martin's canteen, where he was liable to find himself sitting next to an African South African with no passport or an English missionary whose colleagues in South Africa were under arrest. The same year, a white South African girl went home after three years worshipping at St. Martin's. "The first few months at St. Martin's taught me something," she wrote to say. "But I still had a long way to go. Nobody rushed me, and for this I shall always be grateful. But it was at the altar of St. Martin's, sometimes kneeling between an Indian and an African that I finally lost my South African racial prejudice." Her enthusiastic optimism on returning home was soon overshadowed by the circumstances that surrounded her, but she succeeded in forming a multi-racial prayer group in South Africa which met on the same day and at the same time as a prayer group attached to St. Martin's, and for a brief moment once a month, determination cancelled out 7,000 miles and a lot of bitterness.

Once a month an international party is held on Saturday afternoon in the crypt. It goes on into the evening, with dancing and singing and talking. Sometimes a steel band plays. Although the party is thrown by the church, there is no creed barrier, and often there are up to 100 people present. Once a week on Friday evenings, the International Club meets to hear a talk or look at photographs or spend the entire evening in hot debate over the future of Britain as a multi-racial society. There is Emanuel, studying for his law exams, and Sogie with his colourful waistcoats, always laughing. Greg, who won't wear his suèdes in the rain, and Vincent, worrying about his latest brief. Good Girl and Falling Leaves from Japan, and Femi, full of charm and marvellous, impractical schemes.

Once a month, people from all over the world resident in London are invited to a Sunday lunch. Fifty or sixty come. The meal may be chicken and rice cooked by a West Indian, chop suey and bamboo shoots prepared by the Chinese, or roast beef and Yorkshire pudding. There is a strange jumble of conversation and laughter:

"But surely you know that bananas and grapefruit grow on trees!"

"In South Africa we cut a circle out of the top of a pineapple and eat straight through, and grapes are sixpence a pound."

"I like resting more than working. I am happy with my feet above my head. It is when I stand up that I fall over."

At tea with one of the congregation on Sunday afternoon, there are sticky cakes and conversation. Eugene from Czechoslovakia, quiet, artistic and poetic, talking about photography, and Tommy the Communist, jumping around in the middle of the room doing keep-fit exercises. At a late three o'clock lunch, West Indian style, the other side of London, there are lessons in cooking sweet potatoes and where to buy black beans at the market. Back at St. Martin's, three o'clock is time for the start of the Cantonese service in the crypt, taken by the Chinese minister, the Reverend S. Y. Lee. His maximum congregation of nearly 200 comes from all over London. 'S.Y.' travels tirelessly backwards and forwards from one end of the suburbs of London to the other to visit his scattered flock. "Respect the rice plant," he says, "and you will be rewarded with plenty of rice grain." One moment he is sitting on the church steps eating grapes—which is all he appears to eat—and writing long letters in the sun. The next he is up and away to visit a waiter who has cut off his friend's arm with a meat axe. Out of the blue he will throw a big dinner party in the crypt and cook an enormous Chinese meal which he calls a picnic. Before he became a priest, while he was working as an executive with the Hong Kong government, he helped to found an orphanage in Hong Kong. The story sounds like an Aesop fable.

"There was no orphanage," he says, "we could not afford one. The babies were abandoned—not so much the boys, because of the value. Boys could be sold for money. We hadn't a penny, but we had the faith and the love and so we had the hope. We started with ten children and not a penny. We started humbly in a mat shed. Then the typhoon came and blew the roof off. So we had a little more money, and we started again, and we built a wooden house, and the typhoon came again and blew it down. We were becoming known because always our house was being blown down. So we had a little more money, and we built a brick house, and that is safe. Now there are two hundred children."

It happened all over again when S.Y. decided to be ordained and come to London to look after some of the 35,000 Chinese people in England. "When I came to England, I started from scratch, as the English idiom says. If there had been space I would have set up home in one of the restaurants. On 20th September 1964, I took the first service in the Dick Sheppard Chapel. We had twelve people—twelve counting me. To start with, I play the piano myself. I announce the hymn, I sing the hymn, I preach and I pray—and only eleven people. But one family tells another. The next week there are thirteen, the next twenty-six, until we have to move out of the Dick Sheppard Chapel."

Today between fifty and sixty people come regularly to the Cantonese services. At the last confirmation held at St. Martin's over 20 members of the Chinese Church were confirmed. In the congregation there are students, doctors, engineers, nurses, restaurant workers, housewives, Roman Catholics, Methodists, Baptists, Congregationalists, Presbyterians, and Anglicans. Sometimes S.Y. invites another member of St. Martin's clergy staff to preach, and no one knows how much sabotage goes on as he translates the sermon sentence by sentence into Cantonese. In return, every Sunday, he joins with the rest of the clergy administering the Parish Communion.

Once a month, a member of the Chinese church who is also on the Church Council, attends the meetings of the International Committee. He is the committee treasurer. The previous treasurer was a Jamaican girl. The secretary is Swiss, and the committee chairman is on the executive staff of Voluntary Service Overseas. A major item on the committee's agenda is to allocate grants totalling £750 to £1,000 each year to projects and people throughout the world. Many grants support missions, hospitals and schools in tense trouble spots: Jerusalem, South Africa and the newly independent African countries where money is too scarce to be spent on any but the people capable of paying good dividends. Personal contact is always maintained to ensure that money arrives where it is meant to arrive. Letters are read out. From Kowloon in Hong Kong:

> I am Fong Choi Kum, and studying at Bishop Hall Jubilee School. I was born in a simple family and live with parents, my younger brother and sister. Unfortunately my father has lost his job as a cashier in a shop months ago, therefore our living becomes much more difficult. I was afraid that I should lose the chance of studying.
>
> Luckily, with the help of the Principal, Miss Bennett, and my form master, I can receive twenty dollars (H.K.) monthly from St. Martin-in-the-Fields. Even though I am not a very clever student, I will try my best to prove that I take seriously your help. Also I look forward to a change for the better in my family, so that the lucky money will be rendered to another fortunate one soon. Your help to me is much appreciated. Thank you very much.
>
> Yours obediently,
> Fong Choi Kum

And from a clergyman in Ingwavuma, Zululand:

> I write to thank you for the wonderful gift you have made to us. We have been in a desperate need of transport which was mostly demanded by the vast distances between the congregation. We have managed to pay the whole sum for the motor bike and have some money left over for maintenance. All this has been due to your great generosity.
>
> The congregation extend their vote of thanks through me. A Zulu recipient will always say "live long".
>
> I terminate with a big thank you.
>
> Yours faithfully,
> Jacob Dlamini

In the London suburbs a West Indian nurse whose training in Wales was paid for partly through the Vicar's individual funds, keeps in touch with St. Martin's and calls in when she is off duty. An African is able to continue with his studies at Exeter University because a grant is made towards his fees. A Barbadian is assisted to pay for his final year qualifying in horticulture. A Kenya chieftain whose son's debts were paid for him after a member of the congregation found him in tears on the church steps, says, "If ever I can do anything for anyone, let me know." A young Nigerian from Ibadan who came to England with high hopes arrived at St. Martin's in despair. He was unhappy and the only hope was to return home, but a ticket cost £200. Instead, he left the offices one day with a reluctant wave and an unforgettable look of apprehension. In one hand he carried a small bag of belongings. In his pocket he had £5 of his own, and a little more from St. Martin's.

> Glory be to God the father! [began the letter which arrived months later]. Glory be to God the Father and to the Son and to the Holy Ghost, as it was in the beginning is now and for ever shall be, the world without end, AMEN.
>
> My journey from London to Ibadan, Nigeria, by road ended yesterday, 9th February, 1970, when I arrived safely and happily. The Lord's grace and mercy was with me throughout in the course of my journey so much so that I have lots of causes to glorify God. Lots of thanks to you for the money which made the journey possible, for your kindness during my difficult days in London. For your perfect understanding of human suffering and kind approach to every problem. May God's guiding light shine brilliantly through your path always. Amen.
>
> I thought of writing you while I was on the way home, but as the Spirit of God had made me bold and soothed my heart that I will arrive safely, hence I postponed it till now. I have lots to thank you for and I will never forget all you have done for me. It helped a lot to reassure me of my faith in Christ. It also served as a lesson that in whatsoever I do on earth, Christ will be my corner stone.
>
> As you know I have made the journey once before to London from Lagos by road. This helped considerably, to the extent that I hardly needed a map of Africa and Spain while making

Young people from Australia, Scandinavia, Africa and countries across the world meet once a week at the International Club held in the crypt

The Soup Kitchen, open in the crypt every Sunday, offers food, warmth and companionship

this last journey. All the same I bought it together with the map of France. The money you gave me, plus the £5 I had with me I used to buy Travellers' Cheques. On the journey I carried a very modest travelling bag which contained my few clothes, first aid, map, tin opener, etc.

I booked at Victoria Station for train and ferry service to Dieppe in France on Saturday following the Friday that I saw you last. From Dieppe and as a matter of fact throughout France and Spain I did not pay a penny for transport. I did it all by lifts—by way of hitch-hiking. I only paid for sleeping accommodation in cheap hotels, pensions and rooms for letting. I paid for ferry service from Algeciras in Spain to Tangier in Morocco. Throughout Morocco I paid for transport services as the lift system is not common at that part of the world. But like a miracle I did not pay for any transport services in Algeria throughout. Even my transport from Advar across the Sahara Desert to Goa in Mali was arranged free for me by a very kind God-sent policeman. He did it voluntarily. I will never know why save that I know God.

From Goa to Ibadan I paid for one transport or the other but I did not sleep in hotels, I slept with fellow Africans who I did not know, but who were very kind to take me in and provide accommodation free for me for a day or two. I did not spend more than two days in a place after crossing the desert till I got home At present I am doing freelance work for the Nigerian Broadcasting Corporation, Ibadan branch. But I have applied to a newspaper for a job and also to the School of Drama, University of Ibadan.

I know, and I hope you know, there is something else besides me. Which means I know I have something the Lord wishes me to do which at present I do not know. So please pray for me.

I am yours ever,

Kunle

Four times a year, a consignment of presents arrives in the Fiji Islands from St. Martin's, via the Red Cross. Each one has a label with a picture on it, tied on with coloured ribbon. Inside are bandages, but the children on the leper colony say they are healed quickly because they have a piece of ribbon to wear in their hair, and they have never seen ribbon before.

When the nurse in charge came to England on holiday, she wrote to ask if she could meet the young people who sent the bandages. When she came to St. Martin's to meet them, she found one was nearly 80, and the rest averaged around 60.

The Overseas Working Party began nearly forty years ago. Two of the present members were there at the start. Today there are about forty members, and they meet for tea and biscuits in the Francis Room in the crypt every Tuesday evening. Some come from as far away as Pinner in Middlesex and Orpington in Kent, and in spite of the buzz of conversation, the output is enormous. Three large boxes of jerseys and dresses, blankets and bandages are given to the Red Cross four times a year, to be sent out all over the world. When a tidal wave hit Pakistan, forty blankets and thirty dresses went straight to the disaster area. With them went disaster kits, Junior Red Cross bags holding the basic necessities: soap, toothbrush and flannel in a plastic bag, a small towel, a comb, a polythene mug and spoon, handkerchiefs, safety pins, string, a sharp pencil and a notebook. With them go three luxuries which are not really luxuries at all: a hair ribbon, a ball and an unbreakable plastic toy. Disaster kits stand by for earthquakes, floods and hurricanes, when people lose everything they have. And to a child with no home and no parents, a toy may for the moment be more necessary than a toothbrush or any amount of soap.

Long knitted bandages are sent to leprosy settlements, and pink and blue baby bags containing nappies, nappie pins, sheets and little coloured cotton vests made from left-over material are sent out to hospitals in Hong Kong, Africa, Cyprus and the Pacific and Atlantic islands for the mothers who have nothing at all. Wherever parcels are sent, there are always letters saying thank you. The vicar in charge of a convalescent home for children wrote to say thank you for a parcel of dresses. "We always think Saint Helena is a forgotten island until we receive the parcel from St. Martin-in-the-Fields," he said.

In the room next to the Francis Room, the first on the left

down the stairs, Joe has his workshop. Joe, the carpenter comes from Guyana. There are a couple of white Grecian busts on the cabinet by the workbench. One wears a cock-eyed halo. A coat hangs on a peg. There are cupboards all round the walls filled with saws and hammers and chisels. When Joe first left Guyana, it was still British Guiana. It was 1951, and he decided to set sail and study engineering in England. "But I don't get preconceived ideas," he says. "I feel disappointment very keenly, and I don't like to feel it. So I don't get preconceived ideas." Perhaps that just as well. For three months after he arrived in England, Joe just studied. Then his money ran out. The Labour Exchange sent him to St. Martin's, and for three years he worked in the day and studied at night. "But it was too much. I had to give it up. I had only two more years to do, then I was going to West Africa—Nigeria or Ghana. But I shall stay here now."

There is a string of work-rooms and store-rooms in Joe's kingdom. The last of the rooms, past where the ceiling drips, is extremely cold and stretches out under the Trafalgar Square pavement. Each room is piled with stacks of indeterminate things with brown paper round them, odd chairs and cupboards and trestle legs, familiar but hard to place. Nobody but Joe knows where anything is. Nobody but Joe can mend a fuse or stop a tap dripping or paint the ceiling. And nobody but Joe would spend an erratic tea-break at ten in the morning leaning against the pillar looking at the pigeons.

London has changed since Joe first came. Twenty years has increased the number of black faces among the sidesmen and in the congregation. The African women who come to the morning services no longer wear their dresses down to the ground, and KBW—keep Britain white—is scrawled on the Battle of Britain posters in the tube stations when they go home. One day in South-west London two youths and a girl came towards a West Indian member of St. Martin's on his way home. They shouted, "Here's one of them!" punched him and kicked him and left him in the gutter with pepper in his eyes and broken eggs seeping into his clothes. "The Christian is commanded by Christ to love his neighbour," said an article in *The Review* later that month. "This is not easy, and it is not to be confused with being fond of a person. Furthermore the command was not to love his neighbours collectively, but each one individually and treat him as he would treat himself. This is the criterion for all human relationships. No group reaction can stand this test because in the end the individual, and he alone, has to decide whether or not to love his neighbour, because only he can do it. It is his love, his neighbour, his decision, and no amount of clever argument is going to change that, nor is it going to change the commandment."

Perhaps the most concrete example of this kind of love in practice can be seen in a big house in North London. It looks very little like love. It frequently looks more like frustration, tension and insurmountable difficulty. But over and above the hot air which is talked about promoting understanding and breaking down barriers, at the Trafalgar House at Willesden, something is being done. It is being done hesitantly. At times it is done mistakenly and in an amateur way. But mistakes are learned from, and amateurs become professional.

It is four years since a group of people from St. Martin's went to look over the big Victorian house. The walls were damp and rain came in the bathroom roof. The garden was a wilderness. But if the situation was fluid, it had potential. With an interest-free loan from the vicar and a loan from Brent Council, it became the property of the Trafalgar Housing Trust, and today, its potential is greater and not only on a material scale.

The Trafalgar Housing Trust was started in 1966, emanating from an idea conceived at St. Martin's. Its purpose is to provide housing for people from overseas where they can live with local people on a basis of security and equality without any religious or racial discrimination; to create an atmosphere in which understanding and integration can take place in an uncontrived way. It took time. For the first few months there was no hot water in the bathroom and builders were still insulating the walls. Two residents stayed the course. "We stayed," says one of them, Andy Balladin from Trinidad, "because we believed in the idea behind the house." Today, Andy is warden.

Words like idealists and dreamers were bandied about, but gradually the rooms were painted and fitted with kitchen corners, cupboards and cookers. The painting was finished and the garden began to level out and rose bushes were planted. On the day when the sitting-room was finished and the International Committee came to tea, the door came off in the vicar's hand, but the house was beginning to look like home.

It is built on the premise that from mutual interest can come mutual understanding. Already there have been tenants from more than a dozen different countries, and at the moment there are African, West Indian, Asian and English in residence. "We are all entirely integrated", says Andy, who has a job with the Brent Council working towards racial integration, "because we are interested in each other. At least once a week we can all get our heads together and have a laugh and a chat and air our views and explain ourselves. Sometimes people are scared to ask questions. This has to be broken down. And this is why a place like this works. Everyone said it couldn't be done, but I have seen it work at home in Trinidad. It is a way of life there, and I feel we have this to give to the world."

It would be easy to visit the Trafalgar House and see the newly painted well-equipped rooms and sense the warmth and intimacy of the yellow and orange sitting-room, and count the whole venture an immediate success. That would be only half the truth. Sometimes there are misunderstandings. There have been failures. "But misunderstandings come about because people don't know each other," says Andy. "West Indians speak English, but with a dialect. The local boys take offence because they don't understand. And newspapers give publicity to the wrong things. People *can* live happily together. Once they begin to understand they want to bridge the gap. And once he's bridged it, a West Indian wouldn't give up his English friend for anything."

This is what the Trafalgar House is for. It is the culmination of a great many of the things that are done at St. Martin's; a manifestation of much of the thinking that goes on there. It is echoing the tentative plans beginning to take shape all over the country wherever there are multi-racial communities. It could be one step forward in the morass of muddled thinking that builds up barriers where there are none, and makes difficulties large where they are small. Lessons have been learned and are being learned. But unfortunately houses don't grow on trees. And neither does money.

It is unfortunate, too, and in a way ironic, that with the introduction of the Race Relations Act, it is impossible to advertise when a vacancy occurs. Because the ideal is to create a balanced multi-racial community, a degree of selection is essential. But selection is illegal.

CHAPTER EIGHTEEN

# BEFORE YOU LET THE SUN IN

mind it wipes its shoes
(*Dylan Thomas*)

Every year members of all twenty-eight countries of the Commonwealth unite in a Multi-Faith Act of Witness at the Guildhall. A representative from each country lays a flag on the dais and readings are taken from the Holy Books of the Commonwealth faiths. But although the Queen is head of the Commonwealth, the service can be held in a mosque, a temple or a synagogue, but not in an Anglican church.

Over four years ago it was decided to break with the traditional Church of England service celebrating Commonwealth Day. "The majority of the Commonwealth is not Christian," says David Daniels, Secretary of the Joint Commonwealth Societies. "We wanted to make the service a reality for everyone." The obvious place to hold the service was in St. Martin's, the parish church of the Commonwealth. Jews, Hindus, Moslems and Buddhists took part alongside Roman Catholics, Free Church, Church of England and Greek Orthodox ministers, affirming the fundamental beliefs about God and man held in common by each faith. The form of service was one originally drawn up by the Reverend Joseph McCulloch, and already used at his own London church. Christ was not mentioned, and nothing was said by a member of one religion to compromise that religion or give offence to another.

As a result, the Vicar was accused of being hypocritical and untheological and selling Christianity down the river, and, following a British Council of Churches resolution, any similar service was banned from taking place in a church building. To many people inside and outside the Church, in

England and across the world, vision had again been baulked by official timidity.

"We are not pretending to any kind of religious unity which does not yet exist," says the Vicar. "We aren't suggesting an agreed common faith at the expense of what is unique and precious. We are simply sharing such things as we do share. Praying together. Affirming our belief that man is made for God and restless till he finds him. With all the muddles and hatreds in the world today, it is inconceivable that we should add to them. This is simply an attempt to join together in certain affirmations about man and God that will stand against materialism in the world today."

The basis of the act, which is afterwards transmitted on the worldwide network of the BBC, is four main affirmations: the sovereignty of God; the dignity and value of every man, irrespective of nationality, race or capacity; the supremacy of love; and the brotherhood of man. Representatives from the Jewish community, from Hinduism, Islam, Buddhism, the Roman Catholic Church, the Greek Orthodox Church, the Church of Scotland, the Free Churches and the Church of England take part. Readings are from the Gita, the Qurān, the Buddhist Suttamipata, and the Old and New Testament of the Bible. At the end, each representative says a prayer of blessing in his own language. The form of service has already been copied in London University, and David Daniels would like to see it used more widely all over the country in multi-racial communities.

Before the first service was arranged in 1966, the Queen agreed to attend because she approved of the idea behind it and she wanted it to take place. "We should seek every opportunity to get to know one another better," she said in her Commonwealth Day message that year. "This is the best way to avoid false impressions and misjudgements. When you know people well, you are unlikely to misunderstand them."

After the service, the Roman Catholic representative, Kevin McDonnell, said, "My first impression was that this was to be no more than a religious action tacked on to a political demonstration. I was completely mistaken . . . it was a profound religious experience." The late Swami Ghanananda, then head of the Swami Mission, called it a privilege to have taken part, and Peter Martinson, a Ghanaian on the staff of U.S.P.G., spoke of it as "a service with a challenge and a missionary message which many do not yet understand, but may in time".

Evidently the message hadn't reached the members of the Faith and Order Department of the British Council of Churches. They condemned holding such a service in a church on the grounds that it was syncretism—attempting to blend differing religions into one—that it equated Christ with other religious leaders, and that it was liable to offend.

"I believe," says the Vicar, "that Christ sums up all the truth we yet have about God. But I also believe that God is speaking in every religion. This service is a breaking down of barriers; an opportunity to talk and reason together and to learn mutual respect—and that can be done without pretending we are one. The Commonwealth enables people of different colour, faith and race to share some kind of common life and conception of government and law. At a time when the world seems in danger of being divided into black and white, this is worth preserving. I believe that a vast body of people making a stand and witnessing together to man's value and God's care could make a powerful difference in the world today.

"That sounds idealistic: we are in the remarkable position of having representatives of the Islam and Jewish communities both reading from their scriptures in the same place at the same time, when they are fighting tooth and nail in Israel. But we are trying to arrive at the point where certain values are shared so deeply that nothing divides them."

"Love is not arrogant," asserts a New Testament reading in the service. But the Establishment of the Church of England doesn't always fall over itself to prove the point. To revert to the original Anglican-orientated service would have yielded imagination to blinkered expediency. The 1967 service was cancelled, and in the following year, it was held at the Guildhall. "The Queen has attended twice," says David Daniels, "and that says something. . . ." But for the moment, in a world already ruled by divisions—black and white, management and workers, haves and have-nots—this attempt to unite is looked on with embarrassment and suspicion, as if God cannot take care of himself.

There could have been defiance. The service could have continued to be held at St. Martin's, as everyone behind it is convinced will one day be possible. "But I don't want to be a breakaway church," says the Vicar. "I want to have the Establishment with me. I want to hold the service in church because if it is disallowed, it seems as if it is in some way second class, and I don't believe that it is. I want to hold it in church because I think this is something we can pray about.

"When Christ died, the veil of the temple was torn in two. The partition between the holy and the unholy was destroyed. I believe we can meet those with whom we disagree, even in the holiest place. I believe God would permit it. I believe he would want it."

"Be quick in the race for forgiveness from your Lord," says the reading from the Qurān. "And for a garden whose width is that of the whole of the heavens and of the earth."

CHAPTER NINETEEN

# AND THE LETTERS

Capt. Jack Terry,
On board M.V. *Strathardle*,
Kobe, Japan.

. . . My ship was in Shimizu, a small port on the south coast of Japan, notable perhaps for its situation almost at the foot of the very beautiful Mount Fuji. It is not a part of the world notably good for receiving the BBC overseas programmes and I had tried tuning in several times before dinner without any success. After dinner I decided to try once more, and lo and behold, you were coming through quite clearly despite background static. God was on your side as far as short wave reception was concerned for almost immediately after the conclusion of your service the programme faded away completely!

My wish would be to attend St. Martin's more often, but my leave between voyages is short and only a long leave, about once a year, gives me that opportunity. Nevertheless, I feel a part of your congregation on the occasion each month when I listen to your BBC service.

Charlestown,
Nevis, W.I.

. . . I am a regular listiner to your Service. I have Taped your service which are very inspiring and it make me feels very happy to listen to Your services thank You for all those lovely sermons I am asking You to Pray for me in all of your services.

Thanking You in advance

Parana,
Brazil.

. . . Your Reverence I would like you to know, I have the pleasure of hearing your Divine Service from St. Martin's-in-the-Fields, many years now. I am always happier when it comes. I am an old great grandmother 91 years of age. I was born in Oxfordshire, and came to Brazil in 1910. I would like you to see a little of the town I live in. My house is in a straight line to the Cathedral.

Yours very respectfully.

Bangalore,
India.

. . . You are very much in my mind because I always say a word of prayer because you do so much for needy hearts and may God bless you for the work you are doing. Thank you very much for the magazine. I can imagine myself in dear St. Martin's. I used to kneel always in the third seat on the left side. I can picture myself every week day attending the lovely evening service, saying my prayers before I caught the number 68 bus to Herne Hill.

I can imagine myself back again in St. Martin's on Thursday the 18th December, 1952. The schoolchildren were having their Carol Service at 9 am. I was coming back to India that day. My train was leaving from St. Pancras railway station at 10 am. and I still in the church listening to the children's voices. I was able to get a taxi providentially and just caught the boat train as the gates were closing.

I have just returned from staying at a small hamlet several miles away from here consisting of less than a dozen huts all of mud. I lived for almost eight weeks there, doing my own cooking, going to the weekly market and buying my wheat flour and rice, eggs, chickens and kerosene oil, for I had only a small lamp with a chimney for light. I enjoyed being with nature, seeing the rock snakes and King Cobras, the wild elephant and deer. I had my transistor with me when in the village and I was able to tune in to your evening service. I know many like myself wait for your monthly talks over the air, especially we who have knelt in St. Martin's. May you be blessed with long life to spread the gospel of peace.

By God's grace we are having good rains. My mud hut was nearly washed away.

Illinois,
U.S.A.

. . . We sail September 3rd and land in Southampton September 10th. We take the boat train right onto London, and then the fun begins . . . first over to St. Martin's to meet our pastor in England and then to Hatchards at 187 Piccadilly to look at some first editions. . . .

Bombay.
India.

. . . I have entered for the Overseas Listeners Competition for the World Cup. I have to predict (a) who will win the World Cup this year, and (b) by how many goals. If my entry happens to be the all correct one I will win a prize of an All-Wave transistor. If I am lucky this year my worries of going in for a new powerful set will not arise. Padre are you an ardent football fan? If so could you be good enough to pass me on your knowledge so that I could fill in my entry according to the expert's advice? A few tips in your reply will undoubtedly be of immense value to me so that I can fill in the margin of victory as accurately as possible.

God bless you.

Warsaw,
Poland.

. . . I intended to write you some words long ago and today, having more time than usually I sat down and took the pen.

Whenever I can listen to BBC on Sundays I always wait until any mass is on. You may be surprised but especially masses broadcast from Anglican churches I like the best. There are many things in them that make me gayer, happier, less moody.

When I listen to the masses you conduct, father, I always find something new that I found worth to include into my life philosophy. There is something else I feel—I feel encouraged, feel strong, not alone to be a good man, to be so just as God wanted us to be. Through them I fell we all Christians are a large family, great power to face the wrong (or at least it is only my very own feeling).

Thinking that in England as well as in other countries there are people that do listen to services does fulfil me with new energy and deeper understanding. You, father, speak so much of love, love that is lacked in our times. I saw that some of people are afraid of showing off that feeling. Anyway, I agree with you that we ought to see the others not as something that has to exist with us but we ought to see them in our life. It has to be as you said genuine feeling.

All the problems you talk about are very interesting to me. Well, I feel a bit silly because I don't have friends down here that would like to discuss this matter. I feel a bit isolated but anyway I promise to keep listening to your services. Let me finish and wish you all the best, the very best for your efforts to bring nations together under God's crown.

Guyana.

. . . I hope you are well and please say hello to all the folks of St. Martin. Rev I would like to know you by your photograph so please send one when it is convenient. I want to show my friends in Guyana. The sun is very hot at this time and sometimes the heat is terrible. When I want to hear a fine sermon I just listen at St. Martin.

Bye.

Chapultepec,
Mexico.

. . . My husband and I were listening to your services on the wireless last night from St. Martin-in-the-Fields, and we wanted to tell you how very much we look forward to these services. When we listen to them, my husband, who is totally blind, is so absorbed, and tears come into his eyes sometimes. We especially like your sermons. You seem to know exactly what people need these days and they are so human. We just sit quietly and think after the services and they are such a comfort to us both. My husband is Church of England and I am Roman Catholic, but after all, we are all going the same way and there is only one God.

If you ever have a moment spare to write to us, would you mention that I told you that my husband plays, or rather played, the piano. He is a wonderful musician, but on account of his poor sight, the occulist did not allow him to read music, but he has played by ear for years. Unfortunately lately he does not seem to want to play. It makes me feel sad, but he says he does not get the same pleasure out of it. But it would still be a means of expressing himself, and a pastime.

Chapultepec,
Mexico.

. . . It was more than kind of you to write to me and I want to thank you very, very much for your nice letter. . . .You will be glad to hear that my husband has played the piano a few times since. . . .

North Carolina,
U.S.A.

. . . I hear the service every time it is on BBC. I listen to that program very regularly. The only problems are in the transmission. Sometimes it is very bad. Since I am an Episcopalian I have no trouble with the service. Your choir is excellent. I can relate and take part in it all but I like the music best. All sermons, yours included, leave me cold.

Torremolinos,
Spain.

. . . Enclosed please find £1 note to be put to one of your church funds, whichever you may choose. On Sunday last my husband recovered consciousness on the very moment you were speaking on the radio and he just said 'The Vicar of St. Martin's' and afterwards, 'Take up thy bed and walk'. This was a great moment in our lives and will always be a treasured memory of St. Martin's we knew so well when we resided in London.

Tanzania.

. . . It was lovely to feel so near you all, sitting here in my little bungalow on the slopes of Kilimanjaro. In the early twenties we felt all the 6,000 miles away, but today very close. . . .

Praha,
Czechoslovakia.

. . . I regret I am worrying you too much with letters, knowing very well the very serious situation in which you are about work. But then, as a Good Shepherd all the sheep which runs into your pen must be listen to. . . .

St. Lucia,
W. Indies.

To the Reverend Father Fields
Greetings in Jesus name.

I am a member of Christ church, St. Lucia (Anglican) also a constant listener to your monthly services.

I am asking you to remember us here at Christ Church we are very few in number, but trying to be faithful, if I may say so.

Also pray for me Gwendolyn and my Husband Leonard Braithwaite, also my nephew Patrick who is a server. Our parish priest is Father Bebee of Canada.

Thanking you in advance
Yours faithfully,
Gwendolyn, Leonard, Patrick.

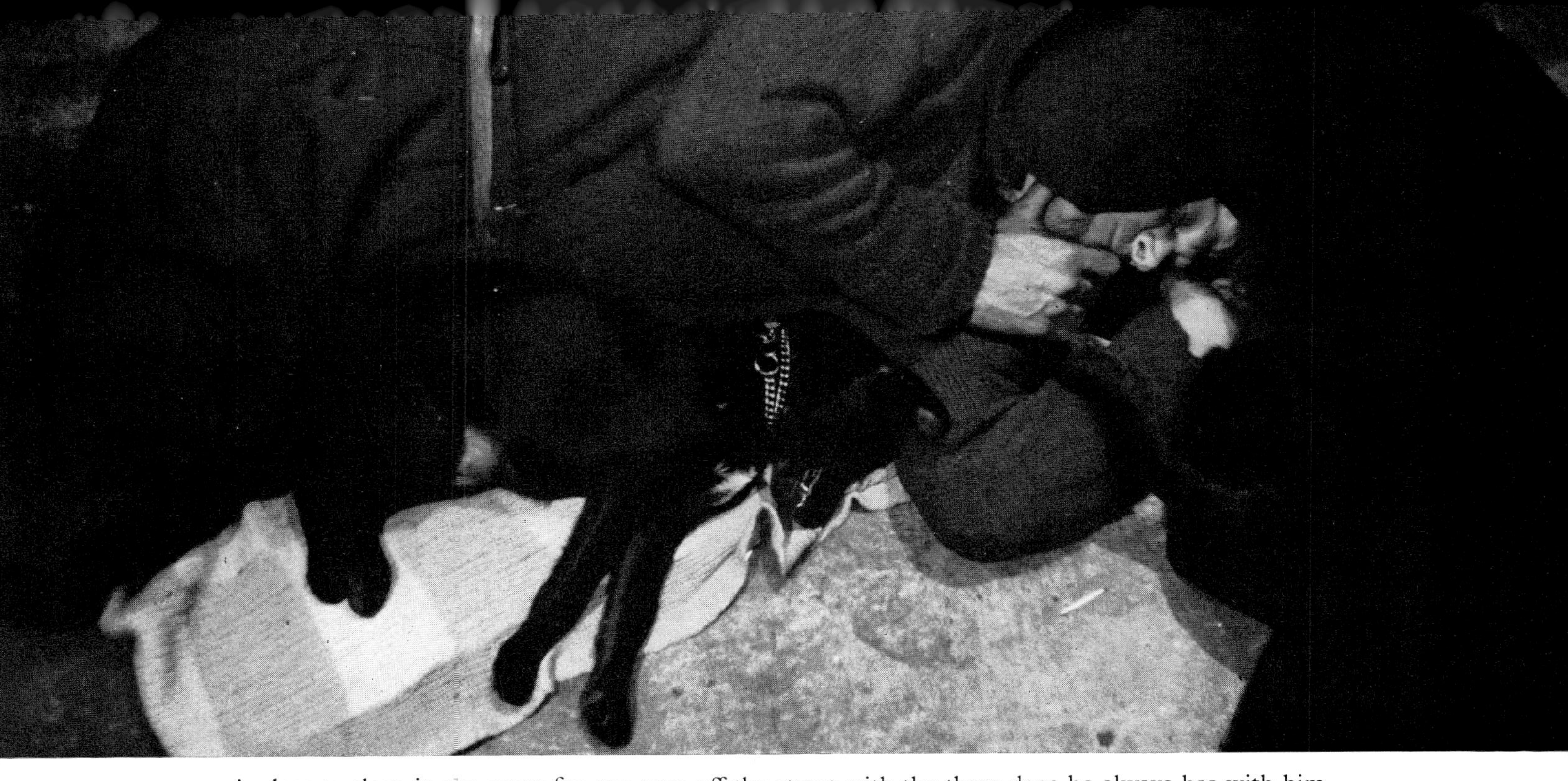

A place to sleep in the crypt for one man off the street with the three dogs he always has with him

Two friends of St. Martin's

Provincia de Lerida,
Spain.

. . . Every month I have the great pleasure to hear the service from St. Martins in the Field, and last Sunday was no exception. Reception was perfect. The acustics are perfect combined with the beautiful singing of the choir shows what splendid choir-master please thank and congratulate him.

I am a retired Englishman from Bradford 75 years married to a French lady. I have worked as Hydro Electro Engineer for mor than 50 years in this lovable country whose people are its greatest asset, I am fortunate to continue to live on where, I have worked and live in the same residence which to me is an earthly paradise.

I thank God for the B.B.C. and the wonderful services they give us throughout the world a you will understand this—when I tell you that I lost my sight totally two years ago.

I have a good wife who looks after me well and am in very good health and I thank God for a most enjoyable life.

Please excuse any faults because this letter is dictate letter by letter word by word to my secretary who does not speak English.

Ouarzazate,
S. Morocco.

. . . I am one of your very big overseas congregation. This letter is just to tell you what a help and encouragement the monthly service from St. Martin's is, and I look forward to it greatly. Sometimes, if not free to listen in in the morning or at 5.15., I set the alarm and tune in at 1.15 am. when there is often a repeat. I know that was the case last Christmas Eve and the Christmas service meant so much. Except for three or four interested Moroccan girls I was the only Christian here but most certainly did not feel alone. . . .

Calcutta,
India.

. . . The service comes to us here from 10.45. pm. to 11.15 pm. which means I am usually in bed and what a wonderful end to the Sunday it makes to hear your message. . . .

New York,
U.S.A.

. . . Reception was absolutely marvellous for the last service of the year here in the U.S. at up-state New York, Oneonta. We were buried (literally) under the worst snow storm since 1888. Over 40 inches of snow fell, drifted and generally made havoc of things. We have had two storms since and we are not yet dug out. Anyway, last Sunday saw all church services cancelled and only rescue and assistance vehicles and the like out on the highways. Your service was a joy to us.

A headmistress,
Baghdad,
Iraq.

. . . As I was listening to your words just now I was strongly moved to write and let you know how very helpful they had been to me. This has been a difficult summer here in Baghdad. On June 8th came the evacuation to Tehran along with all other British and American nationals—or almost all. But about a month later the return seemed possible. At least, an entry visa was obtainable, and I decided to try it, for I felt a great sense of responsibility to my Iraqi staff and students whom I had left behind me so precipitously when the 'Six Days' War' struck. What can one do in situations such as these but 'Look to him and trust that one's face will shine and that one will not be put to shame'?

It had been a long, hot summer of uncertainty and tension in Baghdad, and at times one might be tempted to wonder what good one's presence can do here anyway. And then comes the inspiration of a message such as yours today, and the strong conviction that among a people defeated and struggling such as those among whom I live, one can best serve just by 'looking up to him' with 'courage, gaiety and a quiet mind,' ready to befriend the younger generation and their bewildered parents when the time comes for the re-opening of the school in September. . . .

Puerto Cabezas,
Nicaragua.

. . . I am asking of you a favour. I would like to have all your sermons for the year you see, we could read them over in our services down here. Our people will be very glad to hear them. They are a tremendous inspiration to my family and our friends . . . and, Rev. we will be more than glad if you could kind of adopt us and our little church down here. . . .

Illinois,
U.S.A.

. . . There are plenty of beauty and thrills in life if you look for them. Last evening as we were enjoying our Sunday night supper my English born wife, but now an American citizen, said let's turn on short wave located on the window ledge in our dining room. She did, and it was the re-broadcast from London of the service in St. Martin-in-the-Fields.

What a thrill, so we got out our prayer books and followed the service as many of the prayers in the English prayer book are the same as our American Book of Common Prayer. And, to hear you preach again, well it was a thrill. It was all a ray of sunshine after a rather dull day.

Argentina.

. . . the town we live near is a country town in the centre of B.A. province. It lies 300 kilometres South from the city of B.A., the chief port and federal capital of the republic. We are some 15 kilometres from a paved road. It is when it rains that we know what isolation can mean. There is no postman, and we have not yet been able to instal electricity, and have no chance at all of having a telephone. Ask me what I consider the greatest invention of late years and the answer would probably be the transistor radio.

Bangalore,
S. India.

. . . it is nice to be away from the noise and bustle of the city and here I am at the foot of one of the lesser hills in this state, in an old hut with a damp mud floor and a rickety coil rope cot to lay my head and sleep. It is now almost 11.15 in the night and I will be getting the sports Round-Up from the BBC on the Japanese transistor my younger son presented me with for he knows I go out so often in the wilds in the execution of my duties.

It was a great blessing indeed two Sundays ago to get the service from dear St. Martin's and to hear your voice, prayers and hymns, and last not least, the prayer before the Benediction. My two sons and my daughter-in-law all wish me to say they tuned in as well and were greatly blessed. Like me they also joined in the worship. I am happy, Sir, and may God bless you, my children are coming so close to God by your sermons. Message would be a better word. Like many hundreds, my children and I are greatly blessed.

My daughter-in-law who is a doctor in Madras says every time she attends a fresh case she says a word of prayer. Her husband, my big boy, has ceased to scoff. There is perfect understanding and peace in the home, and no matter how tired the three are they always attend the family altar. Sir, this is what your radio messages have done.

Basseterre,
St. Kitts.

. . . I take great pleasure in writing these few lines to you, hoping when this letter reaches you it might meet you enjoying good health. Dear Rev. we Two always tune in to your service in England to St. Martin in the field and we enjoy your service very much.

Dear Rev. please remember us in you praise we bouth are Methodist we attend church often, so please pray for us, and may the good Lord of heaven guide you and strengthen you to preach the gospel, please pray for us myself and husband, and all who needs prayer, may God bless you as our loving minister I close with love.

Casablanca,
Morocco.

. . . I am sure you will be interested to hear that your service broadcast over the BBC last Sunday came over the air perfectly. I sat in my library with my RGD radio in addition to a zenith portable and the reception was almost stereophonic.

Quite apart from the excellent reception, the service itself was inspiring and indeed, as is the case of all your services, it gave me great pleasure. On occasions, I listen to your services whilst driving my car around the Moroccan countryside, the reception from my car radio being perfect. . . .

Buffalo Range,
Rhodesia.

. . . On a recent Sunday evening, by good fortune I tuned my shortwave radio to the BBC program in time to hear your sermon and the service from your church. In the larger sense I suppose that the word of God needs no fan mail. Rather it is to be hoped that listeners will give heed and practise it accordingly. Yet the human links in the chain may welcome an occasional expression of 'well done', particularly since their utterances carry far afield, and the effect upon distant listeners is normally unknown.

Speaking as one of the countless people who undoubtedly heard you on that occasion, may I say that I was deeply moved by your sermon and by the rest of the service. In an era replete with things that are, in a word, unfortunate, the matter of sending your service around the world is a most fortunate event. Please accept my thanks and good wishes.

Bishopsholme,
St. Helena.

. . . As I listened to your service last evening I resolved to write just a note this morning, although with only a monthly mail ship to this island it will be a long time before you receive it! You bring us a great deal of inspiration and more than any of the Sunday broadcasts. And last month I was so amused to hear a door open and at that moment a siren from a passing ambulance dropped in as a further reminder of a beloved London! I went on after listening to you to preach at my little cathedral and the Vicar had also listened to you and we talked of what you had said. So this brings an appreciation from a good many listeners in a remote island in the South Atlantic where 9190 of the inhabitants are *nominally* Anglicans. Pray for us!

A blessing to you all,
Yours very sincerely,
X Edmund St. Helena.

Moscow,
Russia.

. . . I am a Georgian now living in Moscow. One is to live here to understand how much means your sermon to me, which I listen on BBC. I dream when I'll be able to come to your cathedral to see you and to have your blessing, Father Williams, is there not a possibility to have you more often on BBC. In this materialistic world BBC is not an exclusion it gives very little time to religion, not understanding how necessary it is in our circumstances.

Praia,
Cape Verde Islands.

. . . Greetings in our Saviour's name! On Sunday afternoon, Mrs. Eades and I were resting after having led an open Sunday School at 9.30 and preached in the Worship Service at 10.45. in the church of the Nazarene, in S. Maria on the Island of Sal in the Cape Verde Islands. While resting we tuned into the BBC and were fortunate enough to get the monthly service from St. Martin-in-the-Fields, London, of which you evidently are the minister.

As we listened to your message or sermon our souls were

blessed. I hastily took down some notes, but of course not expecting such an opportunity I missed quite a bit. I am wondering brother whether or not you could send me a copy of your sermon, for I am scheduled to preach at our church assembly in July, and the theme of the assembly is 'GIVE ALL'. Your treatment of this subject so pleased me that I feel that I could pass it on to the National Ministers here and let it be a blessing to them also. Of course it would be preached in Portuguese as this is the language spoken in these islands. . . .

Basseterre,
St. Kitts.

. . . Greeting in the name of Jesus. I am writing to you to let you know how much your Broadcast means to me O how I get a Blessing from it. As you were speaking about grace. We in these days need grace, faith in these days which we live in and the only one we can look to is the Lord Jesus Christ for he give us these things day by day as long as we come to him and give our self to him for he came into the world to save us from our sin. May God keep you to Pour out the message to hungering in need hour. I must also say My age is 19.

Basseterre,
St. Kitts.

. . . Greetings in the name of Jesus. First I must a sorry to keep this letter so long as the season were coming on I had to work so late day and night. I was very glad to hear from you. You mentation in the letter that you would like to know what kind of work I does. Well I must say I does woodwork such as we make Furniture and we also do Funeral Undertaking. Now I must close hope to hear from you again and wish you and your love ones happy New Year in the Lord Jesus Christ and that he will keep you to carry on his good work.

Serangoon,
Singapore.

. . . I do hope this reaches you as I don't know the correct address. I feel I have to tell you how much I enjoyed your Christmas Eve service which I picked up on the BBC World Service this evening.

Being Christmas our thoughts are of course with our families at home, and hearing the beautiful singing from your congregation took me for a short half hour back to cold England. I was feeding my youngest child at the time and thinking of my husband who is at sea off Aden with the Royal Marines until the middle of February. I can't really express how I felt but I just wanted you to know that at least one person many thousands of miles away heard your voice and thought of the true meaning of Christmas.

Capt. Taylor,
M/T Nanyang,
c/o Ocean Trading Co. Ltd.,
Chiao Shang Building,
Hong Kong.

. . . I am writing from my ship which is at present in the port of Tsamkong in China. My ship is permanently employed on the China coast trade and so, except on the odd occasions when we visit Hong Kong, I don't have any chance to go to church. I like, whenever possible, to listen to the Sunday service, and now being in port I could do so, sometimes when we are at sea I cannot because I have to be on the bridge.

One thing I would like to mention and that is the singing of 'O little one sleep' with Bach's music. I thought it was very beautiful. It was also very nice to hear 'Hark the herald angels sing'. I suppose, like many people, this is one of my favourite Christmas hymns. Christmas on the ship was rather quiet as I am the only Englishman on there, everybody else is Chinese. So you can be sure that you have one regular listener out here, and I hope this will be so for many years to come.

Puerto Plata,
Dominican Republic.

. . . I am very glad to inform you that during the closing year I listened each month to the religious services of St. Martin-in-the-Fields, broadcast in the world service of the BBC. These services I have enjoyed very very much and your sermons have been comforting to my soul and have strengthen my faith more in our Lord.

As it is difficult to send money out of this country I am trying to get American money bills in the black market to renew my subscription of St. Martin's Review. . . .

CHAPTER TWENTY

# JEROME AND LENA

Jerome comes from Port Harcourt in the River State of Eastern Nigeria which was once called Biafra. Asked point blank he will not call himself a Nigerian, but an Ibo. He is a member of the English Bar and on the Church Council of St. Martin's. Three years ago he was in prison in Lagos with very little hope of release. Living in North-east London with his Jamaican-born wife Doris and their two boys, he says, "If it wasn't for St. Martin's, I'd be dead."

Forty-four-year-old Jerome first came to England to join the Royal Air Force. "You will laugh at this," he says, "but I was so cold that I slept in full uniform with my boots on." Impeccably polite, with the kind of pride peculiar to Africans, he has a sense of importance characteristic of an Ibo. Two dates are marked clearly in his diary for 1950. "Saturday, 19th June—arrived in England" and "Sunday, 27th June—worshipped at St. Martin-in-the-Fields."

After five years in the Royal Air Force as a telegraphist, Jerome started to read for the Bar. He then decided to return to Nigeria. "I felt there were great opportunities there. When tribal wranglings and killings began to take place, I didn't want to give up my job. The Federal Government said that any law-abiding citizen who wanted to remain behind would be safe, and so Doris and I decided to stay.

"People were living in fear in Lagos at that time. The soldiers were shooting and killing and when Biafran planes bombed Lagos, it grew worse. There was a series of explosions up and down the city, and they began arresting anyone from the East under suspicion. We didn't know who was going to be arrested next. I don't think my children will ever get over what they saw. John was just gone five. He still cries a lot, and he's only eight now but his hair has begun to go grey.

"I was in my office one Saturday. It was about half-past twelve, towards the end of the morning. It was a very hot day, and I sent two of the boys in the office to take files down to my car because I had some work to look over. It was too hot to work any more. I could do them at home in the evening when it was cooler. One of the boys came back to the office and said there were four men to see me. They came in and showed me their cards. They were police officers.

"I asked if I could do anything to help them, and they said no. They said they wanted a chat with me at the police headquarters. I thought they couldn't have come to arrest me. I hadn't done anything—I just happened to come from Biafra. I said, 'What do you want me to come to the police station for?' They said, 'Never mind—when you get there you'll know.' I asked if I could go home first and tell Doris, but they said, 'Nothing will happen to you, so you don't need to see your wife.' I handed the key of my car to the office clerk and told him to take it to my brother, and then I went with them. They still didn't say I was being arrested. They took me to a cell and left me there without questioning me or accusing me or telling me when I might be released.

"I can't describe what it was like. I suppose wherever you are, war is unpleasant. When I remember, it makes me bitter. There were many of us lying down on the bare floor. There was nothing to sit on, and I couldn't eat the food we were given. I hadn't eaten the food the Nigerian villagers eat for years, and I was no longer able to eat it. For four days I lived on water and then a police officer went out and bought me some bread. He was a Nigerian from Lagos, and I have no idea whether he is alive or dead now, but later he came to see me in prison. He took letters to my wife, and I will never forget him as long as I live.

"After a week, we were taken to the prison, and six of us were put into one of the death cells meant for a single prisoner. There was no ventilation. The lavatory was in the cell. There were only two beds, and there were two people who were badly off, so we made them lie down. There was just the bare floor, and I sat down on the floor with my hands on the walls and I went to sleep.

"So that was it—I was in prison.

"Doris didn't want to leave Nigeria until she knew what was going to happen to me, but she is a British subject—she is naturalised English. Her friends persuaded her to leave, and I smuggled a letter out to her telling her to go. I felt worse when she had gone, but right within me I knew that it was best for her and for the children. At least they would be safe. She has never told me how she felt. We can't describe it. We can't put it into words, we just know our feelings.

"When Doris arrived in England, she went straight to St. Martin's.

"I was in prison in Lagos for three months. Then one day they released me. I didn't know why, and they didn't tell me. It was only months later that I found my freedom was due to the Vicar's intervention.

"I got my visa and I came out. I didn't feel safe until the aircraft took off and left the West African coast. Then I felt free to breathe the air again and to live my life, even though the future was unknown. When I arrived in England I learned how much everyone at St. Martin's had done for Doris and the children. They hadn't stopped at doing the obvious things for us. God had helped us in his own way through them. I felt proud, the next time I went into St. Martin's, and everybody welcomed me. Proud because I was part of a place that could extend such a helping hand. Proud—and yet nothing could really express everything else that I felt. I felt my life had been transformed.

"Sometimes I wish I could go back to Nigeria. My mother and my brother and the rest of my family are still in Port Harcourt, and I would like to see them again. But I don't think there is any future for me there just yet. I don't think the bitterness in me can allow me to feel safe to go back. Here, there is no fear of anyone depriving me of my liberty. Maybe one day I will go home. But not yet."

Lena was born on Nevis Island, where the coconut trees spread along the beach as if they were saying, "welcome, come and stay." It is only 50 square miles. England is more that 50,000 square miles.

She is tall and good-looking, and she comes to St. Martin's to the services and to the clubs during the week. She is quiet and she talks little about herself. Questions are turned back on to the questioner. Poised and apparently self-assured, it isn't surprising to learn that she once took lessons as a model in between typing and serving in a shop. "I didn't continue with modelling," she says. "You never knew what would be expected of you." When she laughs, it is a compulsive laugh, and you have to laugh with her.

"I had no idea what England was like," she says. "We had seasons at home, like you do. We had spring and autumn, and in the summer the sun scorched the whole island brown. In the winter you couldn't go out dancing in the evening without covering your shoulders with a woollen shawl. But you were warm enough in a cotton frock.

"I liked Nevis. I liked the coconut trees and the hot springs where your clothes sparkled new and white when you finished washing, and I liked the yellow breasts of the humming birds flying past the people up in the hills shooting pigeons and cooing doves. We kept pigeons in our back yard at home, and we fed them well ready to eat. I couldn't believe my eyes when I saw them running round free in Trafalgar Square.

"At home they all kept saying I must leave. Everybody else was leaving, and they said I must widen my experience. I was quite happy. There seemed no reason to leave. Then one day, on an impulse, I made the decision. I earned some extra money, and I booked a passage on a boat for England. A month later, I arrived in Southampton. I was 23.

"I had no fears. Before I left home, I had been working for

an English veterinary surgeon. He was on furlough in England, and I wrote to tell him I was coming and to ask him to meet me off the boat. I was very naive. I thought England was like Nevis. You can travel from one end of Nevis to the other in under an hour. I thought going from London to Leeds was like walking down to the end of the town. My family still do.

"The veterinary surgeon didn't reply, but I took it for granted that he would meet me. The boat docked at Southampton, and it was the middle of the night, and I couldn't see anyone. I just stood there with my cases. I had nowhere to go, and no job lined up. I knew no one. And money! I had changed £20 on the boat, and because I was stupid and didn't want to part with it and give it to the Purser for safety, I had it stolen. So I had no money either. Only the climate was on my side. Summer was coming, and with the heat of the West Indies still in my body, I didn't feel the cold.

"There were two other girls like me, with no one to meet them and nowhere to go, and a young man from Trinidad came up on the off chance to see if he knew anyone. Fortunately he found us, and he took us back to the house where he was boarding and lodging and we stayed there for the night. In a few days I found a job as a typist, and I contacted a Methodist church who fixed me up at a Y.W.C.A. in Tottenham. As the days went by, I learned to stop smiling and saying hallo to everyone I passed in the street. I got blank looks and no reply, and there were so many people that I would have been saying hallo all day. But life wasn't smooth.

"I was neither sorry nor glad that I had come to England. I kept looking back and thinking how lucky I had been. I could easily have gone astray or been led into bad company. Fortunately I was protected from that. God was looking after me, but I didn't take him very seriously. I was vaguely aware that I was taken care of, but it didn't sink in. Nothing really sank in. I had the sort of mind that didn't allow anything to penetrate very far. I never felt unhappy. I didn't feel enough to feel unhappy. I was very flighty, and I think God said, 'Now I'm going to wake you up!'

"It was as if a bomb dropped somewhere inside me, and it shattered everything. I found myself helpless and powerless, with no control over what was happening to me. I couldn't be bothered to keep myself or my room clean. I had friends, but they were praying friends, I suppose. They didn't come near me very much. I managed to hang on to my job by the skin of my teeth, but I was no better than a tramp.

"Out of that time I somehow woke up to the fact that God was a force to be reckoned with, and not just flirted with as I had flirted with him for years.

"It was about then, at Christmas, that I heard a broadcast from St. Martin-in-the-Fields. I listened to it on my tiny radio, and it made an impression on me. I wrote down the name of the church and the name of the Vicar, intending to send him some money. But I didn't do anything about it. Obviously I wasn't meant to. I was meant to go there in person. One Sunday evening I was standing outside Charing Cross underground station wondering where to go, and the newspaper man said, 'Are you lost?' I asked him if there was a little church anywhere near. 'The only church here,' he said, 'is St. Martin's. If you go up the road and turn left, you'll see it.'

"I don't know why, but I went up the road and in to St. Martin's, and as soon as I went in, there was something in the atmosphere. I couldn't describe it, but it seemed to be alive instead of dead. And as I looked round at the people, it reminded me of the cross. It was like Christ with his hands stretched out. I could see the rich and the middle-class and the poor, the sick, the suffering and the sinning, and those who didn't seem to belong anywhere. There were people obviously at their lowest ebb, living in a different world, without any awareness of belonging anywhere or to anyone. And yet here they were evidently loved and cared for and treated as human beings. In some way they were being fed and sustained, even though they were quite unaware of God's presence around them and with them and in them. They were spiritually dead as I was once, and I could understand them.

"When it was time for the prayers, it was as if God was right beside me. I felt relaxed. I didn't have to pretend. I felt I could be myself and find what I was looking for. I felt I could grow freely without being pressurised, in the way I am meant to grow.

"I never felt that in a church before."

CHAPTER TWENTY-ONE

# THE TWO GARDENS

Thine are all the gifts, O God,
Thine the broken bread.
Let the naked feet be shod
And the starving fed.

There are two gardens in Jerusalem, the Holy City. One is called the Garden of Agony. The other, the Garden of the Resurrection. Tourists, walking the way that Jesus walked, visit both.

Tony has visited them as well. An Arab boy living with his parents as refugees in the Holy City, he knew a good deal about life in the cramped, enclosed atmosphere of the camps. His father died, and his mother collapsed physically and mentally, and because his father had been employed when he died and his Uncle didn't want him, Tony came under no refugee scheme. He was bright. But without training or education, he had the future of a beggar.

But Jerusalem is the city of two gardens. An English matron at a boarding house belonging to St. George's School knew about Tony. St. George's, run by the Jerusalem and the East Mission, provides education to G.C.E. level for children of many nationalities. The majority are Arab. Matron paid Tony's fees for a year, and when she retired and the mission found it impossible to scrape together enough money to keep Tony at the school, they contacted St. Martin's for a grant.

The theme is one that constantly recurs. The cramped agony in the oil-press of hunger, war, fear, poverty and disease. And after the agony, in some form or other, the resurrection, with the promise of dawn through the trees.

In Uganda, in the centre of a leprosy settlement, there is a white-washed church with no windows called St. Martin's church. It is called St. Martin's because Sister Jordan who is in charge of the children's centre, wouldn't stop talking about the church she had left in London called St. Martin-in-the-Fields. At the Kumi Leprosy Centre, St. Martin's really is in the fields.

There is a 3 to 4 per cent leprosy rate in Uganda—at the Kumi settlement alone, there are 300 children. It isn't an easy job. It is a thankless one. But Dorothy is plump and undaunted and she laughs a lot. "At first I was repulsed when I looked at someone with very bad leprosy," she says. "Then after six months I just felt so sorry for them. If the nerve supply to the foot is affected, the feet are numb and a man can walk on red hot embers from a fire and not feel a thing. They take medicine from the native doctors and rub it on, and then, as a last resort, when it doesn't work, they come to us." And it doesn't get easier. "A boy of ten went home for the Christmas holidays. He didn't come back for three months, and when he did, he was in a terrible state. His father had kept him at home to help pick the cotton for ginning."

But there is another side to the picture. The patient who stayed after he was cured and is now deputy in charge of the occupational therapy department. The man with stiff hands who sticks a paint brush between his fingers and paints pictures. The girl who may never be cured, who moved to the adult centre down the road, married one of the patients there, and has a healthy child.

"I went to Kumi because I had read about leprosy in books—in the Bible too, I suppose," says Dorothy, who is a trained nurse. "But I've learned a lot since then. I've learned broadmindedness. I've stopped thinking that if someone isn't Christian, he's wrong. I've learned to see the other person's point of view, and to respect it, and to realise that it is often right. But the most important thing to me is that I feel I can really believe in Christ here. There's a piece in the Psalms:

'If I go up to heaven, thou art there, and if I make my bed in hell, thou art there.' That's how I feel here. Even at the worst times—when I go down to hell—there is somebody to help me."

The majority of the children at Kumi are provided for through an adoption scheme run by the British Leprosy Relief Association. Sixteen pounds a year keeps one child at the settlement—clothing, education and treatment. The Friends of St. Martin's association has adopted eight children, and a yearly grant is paid to the centre through the International Committee. Dorothy Jordan works an eleven-hour day, and part of her time is spent writing regular letters to sponsors, telling them of the children's progress. At the adult centre there are 300 more patients. Drugs are ordered from the capital and they come in by the thousand. The lives of the patients are as near normal as possible. Children go to school on the settlement. Men and women work on the compound, picking cotton and fruit. Those who are less able work in the occupational therapy workshop making rush mats and baskets. A man who had his leg amputated makes his own wooden leg and fits it himself.

"A few years ago, patients sat around doing nothing, feeling miserable and looking miserable. Now they talk and laugh." The compound, the small measure of self-sufficiency, the facilities for the least able to be creative—all these things go some way towards restoring something which is very elusive on a leprosy settlement: a sense of dignity. "We never use the word leper. It means social outcast. Quite a number of our staff are cured patients who had leprosy as children, so even they don't like the word." The feeling of dignity is very difficult to instil into people, and bad cases are often accompanied by shrugged shoulders and "Well—what does it matter?"

But there are brilliant flowers at Kumi. The ground is flat and brown, but there is an orchard of orange and lemon and grapefruit trees, and bougainvillea and frangipani have been imported to the gardens. Patients are paid a little money each week for the work they do even if it is only sweeping the compound, and they go to the shop and buy a coloured shirt or a piece of material for a dress.

"They buy something gay, with bright colours, and you see the difference it makes to them. A shirt may only last for a week, but it doesn't matter. It's something. And it's gay."

Soon after the end of the Nigerian civil war, an airmail letter arrived at St. Martin's Place addressed to the Vicar. It was date-stamped Port Harcourt, 26th February 1970:

> A week after my arrival from the rebel-held area, I received a letter from my senior brother Vincent in London that you gave him the sum of £100 to send to me. When I read the letter, I shouted and nearly fainted with joy. I then handed the letter to my wife to read just to make sure that I was not reading something meant for somebody else. But today I write with great pleasure to inform you that the sum of £100 sent to me has been received. Today I regard myself as the richest man in town. You may not believe this, but I want to tell you that the £100 sent to me now is worth more than £100,000. My wife, children, and myself can now boast of sleeping on a bed which we had not the privilege of sleeping on for the past 19 months. We can now change our diet and have three square meals a day. Glory be to God.
>
> We came home penniless as the Biafran money was valueless and we found that everything in my house had been looted. Even the cables used in wiring my house were all removed. In addition to all these losses, I was told that I can no longer continue with my job. You can imagine my state of mind at that material time, but I took courage in the hope that God never forsakes his people. My parents could not help weeping as their immediate bread-winner had lost his job. My wife was equally worried. But I drew her attention to a portion in Hymns Ancient and Modern, number 181, verse four, which reads thus: "Judge not the Lord by feeble sense, but trust him for his grace; behind a frowning providence he hides a smiling face." It was not easy to convince some of them, but my wife who had

always stood by me during trying times felt as I did. If God could spare our lives when we were in the rebel held area, she just could not see how he could forsake us when all our sufferings were over. Our belief in him was soon vindicated through your generous gift to us. Little did we know that while we were moaning and worrying about our future and that of the family here, God was planning for us through you over there. Is it not wonderful? Thanks be to God and you through whom God has saved me and my family from starvation.

It is not possible for me to narrate our sufferings during the past nineteen months. We are however grateful to God for sparing our lives, and whatever we must have lost materially, cannot be compared to our lives which have been spared.

May I say once again thank you for the wonderful work God has done for us through you.

Yours sincerely,

Christopher

With money to tide him over the most difficult time, Christopher now has a job as headmaster of a grammar school in Nigeria.

A two-room bungalow with an earth floor built on the steep hillside overlooking the Danube, where wet weather sent rain flooding through the door; a refugee called Josef, an old man from Yugoslavia; an Austrian wife and four children, all suffering from TB. A different situation from the lonely refugee families suddenly cast off from the crowded security of D.P. camps. Hopelessness and helplessness of a different kind, hampered by ill-health and resignation.

That was the situation seven years ago, when the United Nations Association contacted St. Martin's. U.N.A. had volunteers to build two big, open, airy rooms on to the bungalow and to re-inforce it against the rains. They had part of the money, and St. Martin's provided the rest. Today the children no longer have TB. Together they help their parents to grow vegetables and potatoes and beet. There are goats and rabbits in the yard outside the bungalow. "They are", says someone who knows them, "overjoyed."

On the edge of the Sahara Desert, where the forests of Aleppo pine and needlegrass have petered out to a few distorted skeletons, a shoulder-high forest is growing in the desert itself. There are acacia and eucalyptus higher than your head sheltering the pomegranate and the honey locust trees. Below them barley and beans and potatoes are growing. Five years ago, when they were first planted with plastic bags of earth and sand and humus packed round their roots and reed screens to protect them in the heat, there was nothing but shifting sands and date palms irrigated inefficiently by an erratic water course. Month by month the palms were buried by relentless sand storms. Young people packed up and left for the overcrowded shanty towns spilling over the edges of the big cities, and the old people remained behind, sitting patiently in the sun waiting to die.

Today, men and women are coming in from the outlying desert villages to learn from patient task-masters how to plant and tend and harvest the trees and crops. Children run in and out of the milk bars while their mothers collect powdered milk. The poorest are given clothes, and as the reclamation of the desert goes slowly and painfully ahead—because the climate is capricious and there are disappointments and frustrations and setbacks as well as a sense of achievement—progress is measured in employment figures, in health, and in expertise, as well as in the shadow cast by shoulder-high trees as the sun sets behind the dunes.

It sounded silly when Wendy Campbell-Purdie, the founder of the scheme, first came into the offices and suggested that St. Martin's should help to plant trees in the desert. But today the Vicar is chairman of the Bou Saada Trust, and a plaque of St. Martin's hangs in the desert. Over 100,000 trees have been planted, and when the bad rains came in 1969, almost all of them remained standing because their roots were strong. Slowly, very slowly, the desert is losing the battle.

Because she had only one eye, everybody laughed at the little

Nigerian girl. The children laughed at her at school, and when they met her in the street, they pointed and shouted out. The standard of her work grew worse, and she always looked unhappy. She had no friends, and when she played, which she didn't do very often, she always played alone.

Three pounds 10s. seemed a very small amount of money to change everything by paying to fit an artificial eye.

One night well past bedtime, the Vicar put through a call to Jamaica. He wanted to know whether the Rector of Half Way Tree could make use of several tons of sausages for the St. Andrew's Settlement. When he visited Jamaica later in the year, they had kept a tin especially for him. St. Andrew's Settlement is very much part of St. Martin's. When they knew the Vicar was coming, the children learned a special song to sing. Six years ago, St. Andrew's Settlement was an idea which didn't exist.

It was six years ago that the Vicar was invited to take a mission in Kingston. He preached from one end of the town to the other, and it was not the rich East End churches that caught his attention so much as the open-air services held in the middle of the broken-down huts of the shanty towns. Some were made of corrugated iron. Some of cardboard. The children climbed all over the camera, and were delighted and delightful as all children are. The parents were tired or bored or belligerent. Black may be beautiful, but in Jamaica, black—very black—is poor. Very poor.

At that time, St. Martin's was running an annual Christmas charity matinée with proceeds going always to children. Over ten years thousands of pounds had gone to children all over the world—refugees, Indian villagers, Save the Children Fund schemes. This time, £2,000 went towards starting a basic school, a clinic and a workshop in down-town Kingston.

The Vicar visited Jamaica again recently to preach in the Montego Bay area during the Church of Jamaica Independence Celebrations. Up in the hills behind the rich houses, a street is just a numbered enclosure. "There was a woman there doing wonderful work," he said when he came back. "I think we should do something to help her. . . ."

In Jerusalem today, St. George's School is run in occupied territory. There has been a 50 per cent increase in the cost of living over the last three years, and unemployment figures are as high as the taxes. Tony has left the school, and St. Martin's is helping to pay for a new scholarship. Jack is 15. He belongs to the Syrian Orthodox Church, and his parents found it impossible to pay for his schooling. This year he came seventh out of a class of forty pupils, and his headmaster calls him one of the best all-rounders in the school.

Jack has also known the two gardens of the Holy City, and he has seen Mount Tabor which Jesus saw when he was a boy. Mount Tabor has two names. Some call it the mountain of temptation in the wilderness. Others call it the Mountain of transfiguration.

## CHAPTER TWENTY-TWO

# RUNNING WITH THE TRUTH

"When we have nothing new to add to what Christians have sung or said before, Christianity will stop," says folk writer and singer Sydney Carter. "The truth will still go running on, but we shall be standing still. To keep running with the truth—that is our destiny. It should be our joy as well—a running, dancing, living thing."

When King David leaped and danced and sang to the Lord with all his might, his wife never spoke to him again. But the Lord was with David.

St. Martin's is known as a church with no prospects for an ambitious organist. The accent is always on participation and involvement, and there is no room for anthems or solos except on high days and holidays, and rarely even then. And yet brilliant organists have been at St. Martin's and are there today. The late Eric Harrison the concert pianist who spent two years in the job had a photograph of the organ console hanging in his hall and a picture of St. Martin's on his desk.

"I became aware of a tremendous spirit while I was there," he said once. "There seemed to be a universal guardian angel hovering over the place." He played Bach at Communion and Methody ranters at the evening services. "I've often felt that there isn't enough extrovert joy in church services," he said. "But you can get joy into St. Martin's. You can break through the respectability. There is an enormous union of people when they sing. There is a feeling 'Let everything that hath breath praise the Lord!' Music in a service should convey gratitude. There's nothing so heart-warming when you've rendered someone a service than that they thank you for it and are happy for it. I would imagine the same happens to God."

There is the glorious non-conformist vulgarity of Cwm Rhonnda and the delicate mysticism of Bach. "Music must involve the whole body. Bach is on a level between the intellect and the heart. A rhythmic hymn where you really let yourself go is on the level of the bowel system which is very rhythmic. Both are spontaneous expressions of joy."

"A church must have beauty," says Robert Vincent, the present organist. "Beauty inspires men. But it must have human warmth as well. I think it is possible to have both."

Nearly four years ago the first Folk Service took place in the church on a Sunday afternoon. It was the first time the singers had sung in a church and the first time the people listening had clapped in a church. But perhaps most remarkable of all is the variety of people who attend the services and the tea downstairs in the crypt afterwards. There are the young and the not so young, the gangs and the lonely, the poor and the well-off, the smart and the scruffy. It has been called touching the hem of worship.

There are no prayers and there is no address. God is often un-named but he is not unsung. He is the maker of the mountain, the creator of the tree. Jesus is the answer to it all. Folk songs are interspersed with poems of men enduring life under the curious stars, and extracts from Martin Luther King, Malcolm Boyd, Che Guevara or a daily newspaper. The most regular performers are The Settlers folk group, who first met St. Martin's when they came to sing on the steps to raise funds for Christian Aid. "You can always give a scientific explanation why things tick," says Mike Jones, their leader. "But in the long run there has to be something that sparks it all off—and this is God. This, to me, is all that matters. That God exists. I don't know in what form. That's not possible for me or anyone else to conceive. But the system works. The human mind is limited: I wouldn't even try to understand what God is really like. Except that he is. That's what matters."

And so at 2.30 something happens in the church which many people would hesitate to call worship. And yet it is a situation in which the truth goes running on with a good deal of noise and enthusiasm and spontaneous gaiety to give wings to its feet.

It is interesting that it was St. Martin's that Kurt Kettner, an Austrian stamp dealer, chose to pioneer his first Music Without Distraction concert, giving stereophonic concerts at little or no price in a darkened church with lights trained on the altar. His thesis is that everyone has within them the facility to reach and enjoy God. "Music", he says, "is something you feel. You cannot put it into words. God gave music to mankind so that mankind could find his way through music back to God. Music is the most important way of touching the human heart. It is the most important way of touching the soul."

> Everyone suddenly burst out singing;
> And I was filled with such delight
> As prisoned birds must find in freedom. . . .

Siegfried Sassoon's words, read out at a concert of poetry and music in the church one Sunday evening. "Music", says Robert Vincent, "should be done, not just talked about." His words echo a tradition set by Jack Churchill, organist and choirmaster at St. Martin's for the nineteen years before Eric Harrison. He left behind him a built-in belief that musically, everyone was able—far more able than they had ever imagined.

With his encouragement, the St. Martin's Academy was formed. Today, they still rehearse, as they did at the beginning, in the drawing-room of their leader, Neville Marriner. Playing music from Handel, Bach, Mozart and Mendelssohn, to Elgar, Tchaikovsky and Stravinsky, their first broadcast was made in the church late at night when the noise of the traffic had ended. Their first record was a collection of Baroque concerts. There was a picture of the church on the record sleeve, and the reviews were good. Today, the Academy has made over twenty-five recordings. They give concerts abroad and in London. A performance of Rossini's sonatas was among the ten best records of 1967. Lively and sparkling in their approach, it is music from young minds that matches their mood most closely: Mendelssohn's String Symphonies and Mozart's Divertimenti, both written when the composers were only 16, and the sonatas which Rossini composed when he was barely 14.

Under Jack Churchill's direction, mid-day concerts were started immediately after the end of the Second World War. Today they are still taking place twice a week in the church. The acoustics are good, and so is the standard of the performers. Programmes range from Mozart to Britten, Faure to Messiaen; from string quartets and clarinet solos to motet choirs. Businessmen come in with their sandwiches, students with their books, shoppers with carrier bags and tourists with maps and cameras. For three-quarters of an hour, work, money and sight-seeing are forgotten. "It is a different world," said a businessman.

> Everyone's voice was suddenly lifted;
> And beauty came like the setting sun:
> . . . O, but Everyone
> Was a bird; and the song was wordless;
> the singing will never be done

The pointing of a psalm, unstructured blues, the explosion of glory when a symphony or a sonata touches its highest moment: each is in its own way a kind of worship. In the crypt at night, coloured lighting, flickering candles, arches and vaulted ceilings make an almost hackneyed setting for a folk club. "It's an ideal hall," said The Settlers one night to an audience of 300 or 400. "There's an even better one upstairs."

"In ballads, blues and cradle songs," says Sydney Carter, "mankind wrestles with reality, joyfully or bitterly, like Jacob with the angel, demanding to be told the name and nature of its maker, of itself. It is a form of praise. A form of worship."

In Holy Week, the folk club came the nearest it has ever come to conventional worship. The story of the Last Supper was read out, and the songs were Easter songs: "Were you there when they crucified my Lord? And the creed and the colour and the name won't matter. Were you there?" A loaf of bread and a bottle of wine were blessed and passed round from hand to hand. There were Quakers and Roman Catholics, Indians and Africans, lapsed communicants, friends and strangers, young people and older people, and the creed and the colour and the name didn't matter because they were there.

The glasses used for the wine came from the pub round the corner, and that was where the evening ended. It had been, as it so often is when folk songs are sung and music is played and people are involved with each other, a kind of explosion: a catharsis of excitement that found its expression in something very close to worship. It was not classical or correct or particularly well-behaved, but when David leaped and danced and sang at the top of his voice, he gladdened the heart of God.

## CHAPTER TWENTY-THREE

# SUNDAY EVENING

"They that wait upon the Lord shall renew their strength. They shall mount up with wings like eagles. They shall run and not be weary. They shall walk and not faint."

Like animated figures flung from a magic lantern the characters gyrate and somersault across the wall. Clowns and tragi-comedians, jerking and convulsing involuntarily to someone else's rhythm. Scapegoats and dare-devils, heroes and unsung heroines, projected shadows in the background.

"Lord, I want to have proper thoughts, religious thoughts, holy thoughts. Help me to stop being stupid. Accept my thoughts as they are. If they are wrong, help me to put them right. If they are confused, help me to straighten them out. If they are right, help me to make the most of them."

There is no creed at an evening service. Those who believe it attempt in their own way to live it. The rest are not yet sure. Like the poet who wrote "We gave to the world one another's best," nothing is demanded but that people should be themselves.

"I have a nightmare," said someone. "I imagine Jesus coming to Trafalgar Square and walking past St. Martin's without noticing it." Michael, chalking contorted pictures on the pavement outside makes it unlikely that the nightmare could come true. So does Paddy, grumbling because his new boots pinch.

"And now may courage, gaiety and a quiet mind and all other gifts from a father to his children be yours. . . ." The service ends and it has been a kind of celebration. Outside, Frank, swearing like a trooper, says, "What the hell was all that about?"

The spirit of St. Martin's has never been pigeon-holed. Like the new wine in old skins, it would be bound to break free and leak in the most awkward places. Stripped of its mystique, it is something very slight: a moment of beauty in the banal, of humour through sadness, a hint of unimagined potential. In the middle of chaos it is an inexplicable pause for understanding. It is the unpredictable in a situation which brings a flash of light where there was unfathomable darkness.

It is the wilderness as well as the mountain top. A little, as he said, like a love affair.

One day there was a man walking round in the crypt with a hat on his head and a haversack on his back, saying he was God Almighty. And in a sense that was what one expected.

# BIBLIOGRAPHY

HUMPHREY, W. G., *St. Martin-in-the-Fields in the Olden Time* (Edward Stanford 1876).
MCMASTER, JOHN, *St. Martin-in-the-Fields* (John McMaster), 1916.
BRITAIN, VERA, *The Story of St. Martin's, an Epic of London*, 1951
TOURTEL, HAZEL, *St. Martin-in-the-Fields—a Short History*, 1964
SHEPPARD, H. R. L., *Echoes from St. Martin-in-the-Fields* (The Athenaeum Press), 1934
*Dick Sheppard by his Friends* (Hodder and Stoughton), 1938
ROBERTS, R. ELLIS, *H. R. L. Sheppard, Life and Letters* (John Murray), 1942
STUDDART-KENNEDY, G. A., *The Unutterable Beauty* (Hodder and Stoughton), 1964
*St. Martin's on the Air*, broadcast addresses by Pat McCormick (The Athenaeum Press), 1936
NORTHCOTT, R. J., *Pat McCormick—A Man's Life* (Longman's, Green and Co.), 1941
LOVEDAY, ERIC S., *A Great View* (Skeffington), 1951